The BRICS: A Very Short Introduction

VERY SHORT INTRODUCTIONS are for anyone wanting a stimulating and accessible way into a new subject. They are written by experts, and have been translated into more than 40 different languages.

The Series began in 1995, and now covers a wide variety of topics in every discipline. The VSI library now contains over 450 volumes—a Very Short Introduction to everything from Psychology and Philosophy of Science to American History and Relativity—and continues to grow in every subject area.

Very Short Introductions available now:

ACCOUNTING Christopher Nobes
ADVERTISING Winston Fletcher
AFRICAN AMERICAN RELIGION
   Eddie S. Glaude Jr
AFRICAN HISTORY
   John Parker and Richard Rathbone
AFRICAN RELIGIONS
   Jacob K. Olupona
AGNOSTICISM Robin Le Poidevin
ALEXANDER THE GREAT
   Hugh Bowden
ALGEBRA Peter M. Higgins
AMERICAN HISTORY Paul S. Boyer
AMERICAN IMMIGRATION
   David A. Gerber
AMERICAN LEGAL HISTORY
   G. Edward White
AMERICAN POLITICAL HISTORY
   Donald Critchlow
AMERICAN POLITICAL PARTIES
   AND ELECTIONS L. Sandy Maisel
AMERICAN POLITICS
   Richard M. Valelly
THE AMERICAN PRESIDENCY
   Charles O. Jones
THE AMERICAN REVOLUTION
   Robert J. Allison
AMERICAN SLAVERY
   Heather Andrea Williams
THE AMERICAN WEST Stephen Aron
AMERICAN WOMEN'S HISTORY
   Susan Ware
ANAESTHESIA Aidan O'Donnell
ANARCHISM Colin Ward

ANCIENT ASSYRIA Karen Radner
ANCIENT EGYPT Ian Shaw
ANCIENT EGYPTIAN ART AND
   ARCHITECTURE Christina Riggs
ANCIENT GREECE Paul Cartledge
THE ANCIENT NEAR EAST
   Amanda H. Podany
ANCIENT PHILOSOPHY Julia Annas
ANCIENT WARFARE
   Harry Sidebottom
ANGELS David Albert Jones
ANGLICANISM Mark Chapman
THE ANGLO-SAXON AGE John Blair
THE ANIMAL KINGDOM
   Peter Holland
ANIMAL RIGHTS David DeGrazia
THE ANTARCTIC Klaus Dodds
ANTISEMITISM Steven Beller
ANXIETY Daniel Freeman and
   Jason Freeman
THE APOCRYPHAL GOSPELS
   Paul Foster
ARCHAEOLOGY Paul Bahn
ARCHITECTURE Andrew Ballantyne
ARISTOCRACY William Doyle
ARISTOTLE Jonathan Barnes
ART HISTORY Dana Arnold
ART THEORY Cynthia Freeland
ASTROBIOLOGY David C. Catling
ASTROPHYSICS James Binney
ATHEISM Julian Baggini
AUGUSTINE Henry Chadwick
AUSTRALIA Kenneth Morgan
AUTISM Uta Frith

Available soon:

For more information visit our web site

www.oup.com/vsi/

Andrew F. Cooper

THE BRICS

A Very Short Introduction

Great Clarendon Street, Oxford, OX2 6DP,
United Kingdom

Oxford University Press is a department of the University of Oxford.
It furthers the University's objective of excellence in research, scholarship,
and education by publishing worldwide. Oxford is a registered trade mark of
Oxford University Press in the UK and in certain other countries

Published in the United States of America by Oxford University Press
198 Madison Avenue, New York, NY 10016, United States of America

British Library Cataloguing in Publication Data

Data available

Library of Congress Control Number: 2015959267

ISBN 978-0-19-872339-4

Printed in Great Britain by
Ashford Colour Press Ltd, Gosport, Hampshire

Contents

Preface

For an invented concept the BRICS has made a serious impact on global politics. Notwithstanding widespread scepticism that a group of non-Western countries, brought together largely by a common sense of frustration with the established rules of the game, could hang together, BRICS has consolidated its club activity since the 2008 global financial crisis. Debate continues on the exact meaning of the forum. What is clear, however, is that the importance of the BRICS lies both as a symbol of and an instrumental vehicle for change in the global system.

There is no lack of commentary about the rise—or putative fall—of the BRICS. Reflecting the theme of transformation in current public debate, an array of investment professionals, journalists, and scholars have made judgements about the phenomenon. However, the bulk of these analyses focus on the economic profile of the BRICS. What has been lacking is a study that highlights not only the economic but diplomatic and geostrategic implications of the BRICS. This VSI aims to fill this gap in a standalone readable format.

To be sure, the BRICS are constrained by numerous internal tensions and contradictions. With a membership that consists of Brazil, Russia, India, China, and South Africa, the BRICS do not possess the coherence of traditional informal institutions made up of incumbents clustered within the G7. Yet, notwithstanding all of these differences, the BRICS have managed to create a sustained club personality. From a low-key consultative site in 2008, the BRICS process has deepened as well as widened. The BRICS summit at the leaders' level has maintained a defensive approach with a reactive culture to the performance of not only the G7 but the G20, the premier forum of economic governance to which all the BRICS members also belong.

At the same time, though, the BRICS has moved beyond the demandeur style associated with earlier challenges of the global South via the campaign for a New International Economic Order. At the summit level the BRICS displays a sense of spectacle and confidence that parallels the practices of the G7. Moreover, with the move to establish the New Development Bank, the BRICS belies the criticism that it is only a talking shop.

Although this progress amply justifies the inclusion of BRICS in the VSI series, the ongoing essence of the forum remains open to question. Can the BRICS be both a vehicle of enhanced ambitions and search for recognition for a select cluster of countries beyond the traditional Western establishment and a means of upward mobility for the 'rest' in the global South? Or does the BRICS simply reproduce the exclusivity built into the status quo? Such a contest plays out as well in terms of its internal dynamics. Started as a state-centric mechanism, the BRICS continues to feature attributes that reinforce this impression. Conversely, there are signs that the trajectory of BRICS is bending its original nature by building in a role for society as well as state-based actors.

If I view BRICS in a generally positive light, as a logical and justifiable response to the patterns of power asymmetries and marginalization of the past, the potential shift of this challenge into the very different—and more alarming—terrain of geopolitical conflict cannot be dismissed. As in past eras, navigating passage between an old order dominated by an established elite and a new system with a greater role for traditional outsiders is highly sensitive, especially when key countries within the challenger group have so very different national political systems. This BRICS VSI therefore is at the core of debates about the future of international relations, not only because of the size and functioning of these economies, but because of the insights they give to the mode of transition in the distribution of status and authority in the 21st century.

Acknowledgements

My interest in the phenomenon of rising powers originated in the time (2003–10) when I was Associate Director and Distinguished Fellow at the Centre for International Governance Innovation. Sparked by a concern about how big non-Western countries could be accommodated into the established world order, I engaged in an extended series of activities about the means to change the global rules of the game.

As my focus turned more specifically to the creation, evolution, organizational structure, type of agency, and overall meaning of the BRICS, I have been fortunate to work with and to gain the insights of a number of colleagues. These included Greg Chin, Jorge Heine, Alan Alexandroff, Ramesh Thakur, John Kirton, Yoginder Alagh, John Whalley, Manmohan Agarwal, Tim Shaw, Hany Besada, and Agata Antkiewicz, as well as Daniel Schwanen and John English.

In a wider network of prominent individuals with a concerted interest in BRICS-related themes I benefited from the expertise of Dirk Messner, Thomas Fues, Heribert Dieter, Paola Subacchi, Tony Payne, Hugo Dobson, Daniel Drache, Dries Lesage, Paulo Esteves, Adriana Erthal Abdenur, Elizabeth Sidiropoulos, Mzukisi Qobo, Su Changhe, Wang Yong, Zhu Jiejin, Marina Larionova, and H. H. S. Viswanathan.

With my return to full time academia in the Department of Political Science and the Balsillie School of International Affairs at the University of Waterloo my research has continued to benefit from interacting with a cluster of respected scholars, notably Eric Helleiner, Jennifer Clapp, John Ravenhill, Kathy Hochstetler, Hongying Wang, and Bessma Momani.

Throughout this entire span of time I received support in a variety of ways from Kelly Jackson, Andrew Schrumm, Max Brem, Dan Herman, and Ben Cormier. I am especially grateful to the varied skill set of Madeline Koch, Asif Farooq, and Warren Clarke who helped complete the book. Madeline smoothened out the stylistic presentation of the manuscript. Asif, who I have co-authored a number of publications with, facilitated the research. Warren not only aided in the preparation of illustrations and tables, but (along with Alan Alexandroff) closely read the manuscript.

The senior commissioning editor of the VSI series, Andrea Keegan, guided me smoothly from the outset of the publishing process. I thank her and her colleagues at Oxford University Press, particularly Jenny Nugee, for their help in ensuring a quality production. The input from three anonymous referees benefited both the original proposal and the draft manuscript.

The responsibility for any errors in the book lies with the author alone.

List of illustrations

List of tables

Acronyms and abbreviations

AfDB	African Development Bank
AIIB	Asian Infrastructure Investment Bank
APEC	Asia-Pacific Economic Cooperation
BASIC	Brazil, South Africa, India, and China
BNDES	Brazilian Development Bank (Banco Nacional de Desenvolvimento Econômico e Social)
BRIC	Brazil, Russia, India, and China
BRICS	BRIC plus South Africa
CDB	China Development Bank
CIVETS	Colombia, Indonesia, Vietnam, Egypt, Turkey, and South Africa
COP	Conference of the Parties to the United Nations Framework Convention on Climate Change
CRA	Contingent Reserve Arrangement
eximbank	export-import bank
FDI	foreign direct investment
FOCAC	Forum on China–Africa Cooperation
G2	Group of Two: China and the United States
G7	Group of Seven (Canada, France, Germany, Italy, Japan, United Kingdom, United States, and the European Union)
G8	Group of Eight (G7 plus Russia)
G20	Group of 20 (Argentina, Australia, Brazil, Canada, China, France, Germany, India, Indonesia, Italy, Japan, Korea, Mexico, Russia, Saudi Arabia, South Africa, Turkey, United Kingdom, United States, and the European Union)

G77	Group of 77 developing countries
GDP	gross domestic product
HDI	human development index
IBSA	India-Brazil-South Africa Dialogue Forum
IFI	international financial institution
IMF	International Monetary Fund
MERCOSUR	Common Market of the South, Mercado Común del Sur
MINT	Mexico, Indonesia, Nigeria, and Turkey
MIST	Mexico, Indonesia, Korea, and Turkey
N11	Next 11 (Bangladesh, Egypt, Indonesia, Iran, Korea, Mexico, Nigeria, Pakistan, the Philippines, Turkey, and Vietnam)
NAM	Non-Aligned Movement
NDB	New Development Bank
NGO	non-governmental organization
NIC	newly industrialized country
NIEO	New International Economic Order
NSA	national security adviser
O5	Outreach Five (Brazil, China, India, Mexico, and South Africa)
OECD	Organisation for Economic Co-operation and Development
ORF	Observer Research Foundation
P5	Permanent Five (members of the United Nations Security Council)
PPP	purchasing power parity
RIC	Russia, India, and China
SAARC	South Asian Association for Regional Cooperation
SADC	Southern African Development Community
SCO	Shanghai Cooperation Organization
UNSC	United Nations Security Council
WTO	World Trade Organization

Chapter 1
Framing the BRICS

The acronym BRICS has become synonymous with a shift in power in the 21st century. Yet, despite its widespread prominence in academic and popular commentary on global economic and political affairs, the nature of the BRICS is not well understood. This confusion stems largely from the multiple meanings that have been attached to the label from the time it was first introduced by Jim O'Neill of Goldman Sachs in 2001. Originally created to highlight a set of similar economic characteristics possessed by Brazil, Russia, India, and China, the acronym has evolved to take on a diplomatic format first as BRIC in 2008 and subsequently as BRICS with the inclusion of South Africa in December 2010. With annual summits at the core of this institutional process, the BRICS has assumed a defined club-like personality with a significant international profile. In terms of substantive collective action, the major initiative of the BRICS members has been the implementation of the New Development Bank (NDB) and Contingent Reserve Arrangement beyond the ambit of the post-1945 international financial institutions (IFIs). These sustained group dynamics have in turn opened up a debate about whether the BRICS poses a geostrategic challenge to traditional Western dominance via a significant reordering of the global system.

Given these different connotations, the BRICS must be analysed using a variety of frameworks. At the most basic and foundational level, the BRICS remains an indicator of the impressive rise in economic size from a cluster of big emerging markets outside the West and, particularly, beyond the traditional powers within the Group of Seven (G7) (see Figure 1).

Publications since the early 2000s have interpreted this evolution as a dynamic and favourable trend driven largely by the BRICS countries' embrace of globalization, complex interdependence, and the achievement of high levels of economic growth. The hallmark of these success stories is the perceived ability of the BRICS to catch up and eventually surpass the established G7 countries in terms of economic and, potentially, political weight. Thus, as early as 2003, Goldman Sachs forecast that China and India would become the first and third largest economies in the world by 2050, with Brazil and Russia capturing the fifth and sixth spots over the same period. The timelines for some of these shifts have actually exceeded the expectations of early BRIC advocates, with China becoming the largest economy in the world in 2014 in terms of purchasing power parity (PPP being differentiated from nominal gross domestic product for taking country-specific cost factors into consideration).

The BRICS concept is thus closely linked to a narrative about the growing economic weight of large emerging market economies. Early accounts of the phenomenon put forward by financial analysts, consultancy firms, and asset fund managers stressed the positive nature of these shifts for both the countries themselves and the broader global economy. Academic assessments, in contrast, have embraced a degree of scepticism about the salience of an investment-marketing concept.

While the growing impact of the individual countries was clearly evident, the BRICS concept as an interpretative device suffers from significant limitations. Indeed, given the economic profiles of

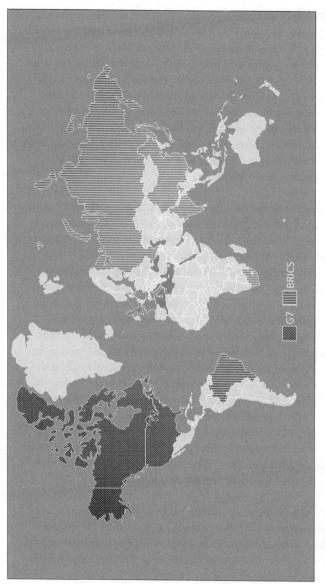

1. The BRICS and the G7.

the BRICS countries as parallel entities, it is the contrasts—rather than the commonalities—that stand out. On almost any criteria related to gross domestic product (GDP), trade, investment, or currency reserves, China performs as a super-BRICS member. Russia, by contrast, is an outlier, depending excessively on oil and gas exports with a conspicuous component of high-end consumers, but little else in the way of a BRICS ascendant profile. In terms of high-growth sectors, China as the 'world's manufacturer' diverges appreciably from India with its technology and 'global call centre' hubs as well as the resource-oriented Brazil and South Africa.

The BRICS concept differs from other labelling efforts to identify the rise of a selective cluster from beyond the West, however, because it translates the original concept into sustained institutional activity. Confined exclusively to a depiction of shared economic characteristics, the BRICS has to ward off the impression that it is a contrived brand, in the mix with a host of other labelling artefacts. These competitors range from the older group of the 'Big Ten' cluster (China, India, and Brazil as well as Mexico, Argentina, Indonesia, Poland, South Africa, Republic of Korea (Korea), and Turkey) identified by Jeffrey Garten, former dean of the Yale School of Management, to newer concepts such as the Boston-based Fidelity Investments' MINT (Mexico, Indonesia, Nigeria, and Turkey), the Economist Intelligence Unit's/HSBC's CIVETS (Colombia, Indonesia, Vietnam, Egypt, Turkey, and South Africa), and even Goldman Sachs' follow-up groups, the Next 11 (N11—Bangladesh, Egypt, Indonesia, Iran, Korea, Mexico, Nigeria, Pakistan, the Philippines, Turkey, and Vietnam), and MIST (Mexico, Indonesia, Korea, and Turkey).

What fundamentally distinguishes the BRICS acronym from its competitors is the ongoing transformation of the original descriptive and predictive concept into diplomatic practice, with the creation of the first official BRICS (or, more precisely, BRIC) summit in 2009. Rather than simply being an artificial invention, the BRICS is a manifestation of the ascendancy of informal operational practices in global affairs. Through the post-1945 era, universal-oriented organizations held dominant sway. It was a central challenge for the global South to win recognition in this set of organizations—thanks to a campaign waged on the basis of fairness with a demand for a reallocation of institutional standing vis-à-vis the West. The demand for reform was particularly intense with respect to the IFIs, where Western control was most firmly entrenched. While a more equitable set of rules in universal institutions remains one of the core strategic objectives of the BRICS, the group's tactical repertoire has tilted towards building capacity through self-selective institutional forums.

If the turn towards informality altered the relationship between the BRICS and the G7, it also created a dilemma within the global South. The descriptive element of the BRICS concept may have showcased the movement of emerging market economies from the periphery to the core of the international system, but the translation of the BRICS into diplomatic practice has bifurcated the global South, opening up a divergence between the BRICS and the 'rest'. The objective of the BRICS countries working together, if commonly expressed in declaratory statements as a means of promoting cooperation within the non-West, is driven by a desire to leverage changes in the institutional architecture to their specific operational advantage.

By the early 2000s, the BRICS gained special albeit uneven access and recognition from the Western establishment. After the shocks of the global financial crisis in 2008, this process of engagement between the BRICS and the members of the G7 was accentuated by the elevation of the finance Group of 20 (G20), created in the late 1990s due to the fallout from the Asian financial crisis, to a G20 summit at the leaders' level.

Although it is true that the BRICS share membership in the G20 with a number of other countries beyond the West (a cluster including Indonesia and Turkey—countries included in a number of acronyms other than the BRICS), the vast majority of the rest from the global South are left out of this newer type of informal institutionalism. More dramatically still, only the BRICS could combine engagement with the G7 countries through the more inclusive G20 forum with autonomous action of their own. Whereas the other members of the G20 from the global South outside the BRICS lack a common diplomatic personality, the BRICS have moved ahead to organize an informal summit process of their own.

Rise of the BRICS

Just as the acronym of BRICS, with its focus on economic parallelism, overlooks individual differences, the framing of the BRICS in terms of operational practices ignores a number of important constraints on members' ability to undertake collective action. The members of the G7 club might differ on specific issues but there exists a like-mindedness that binds them together. All of the G7 countries, whether they possess a presidential or legislative-based political system, operate as free and fair democracies.

By way of contrast, BRICS countries lack this type of common political glue. China, although performing in spectacular fashion with respect to economic growth since the reforms (socialism with Chinese characteristics) introduced by Deng Xiaoping in 1978, continues to be a single-party state. Changes in political leadership occur in a regularized but non-transparent fashion, as illustrated by the opaque procedure involved in the November 2012 election of Xi Jinping to the post of General Secretary of the Communist Party of China. Russia under Vladimir Putin retains the character of a managed democracy, with centralized power that trumps parliamentary politics.

In complete contradistinction, the other BRICS members possess a wide range of vibrant democratic features. India is distinguished not only by the massive scale of its election process but also by the intense competition between its major political parties. Whereas Manmohan Singh of the Indian National Congress was able to form governments in 2004 and 2009, Narendra Modi and the Bharatiya Janata Party won a resounding victory in May 2014. Luiz Inácio Lula da Silva of the Workers' Party (Partido dos Trabalhadores, PT) won the presidency of Brazil in successive elections in 2002 and 2006 after losing three times in 1989, 1994, and 1998. Lula's handpicked successor, Dilma Rousseff, was re-elected in October 2014 after a close contest in which she won only 51 per cent of the votes. Although the African National Congress retained power after the May 2014 South African election, Jacob Zuma and his political party had to contend with a reduced majority (62.1 per cent, down from 65.9 per cent in 2009) and stronger performances from the official opposition Democratic Alliance and the newly created Economic Freedom Fighters led by its firebrand leader Julius Malema.

The major differences among the BRICS countries, with respect to both interests and identities, also stand as important barriers to effective cooperation. Institutionally, there is a marked contrast between the advantages enjoyed by Russia and China in the global system as veto-wielding insiders within the United Nations Security Council (UNSC) and India, Brazil, and South Africa as outside the Permanent Five (P5) members of the UNSC. Moreover, Russia was granted a unique form of compensation in the aftermath of the collapse of the Soviet Union, by its accession into an extended leaders' forum of the Group of Eight (G8), although it was excluded from the G7 finance ministers' forum.

On top of these differences in comparative institutional status, there are other fundamental sources of competition among the BRICS countries. There are sharp legacies of territorial disputes between India and China, as well as between Russia and China. These historical tensions have emerged on a range of issues. India and China, for example, continue to compete over energy sources and supply chains, including the establishment of ports in nearby countries. India is moving to construct the Chabahar project inside Iran, while China operates the competing Gwadar port close by in Pakistan. More directly, China and India have clashed in the Depsang Valley along the border that separates Indian- and Chinese-controlled areas.

To some extent, the ability of the BRICS to overcome these sources of divergence and competition hinges on the animation of a shared symbolism. Reinforced by Goldman Sachs' identification of the countries as a special cluster among the rest of the global South, the BRICS members have defined themselves as not just regional drivers but as global players fundamentally different from other entities in the non-West. Such a privileged casting has fuelled the collective ambitions of the BRICS to take a greater (and rightful) role in the world and, at the same time, to escape the confinement and difficulties of their immediate geographic neighbourhoods. Whatever else divides the BRICS members, they increasingly take the view that they are now too big to play roles only in their respective regions. Only South Africa made a effort from the outset of its membership to place a comprehensive regional agenda—with a specific focus on Africanization—at the core of the BRICS platform.

Idea to institution

The previous engagement of the BRICS countries with the 'G' summitry process has been an important source of shared symbolism, and catalysed the creation of the BRICS summit itself. Initially, the BRICS countries engaged with the G7/8 through the development of the so-called outreach process. The 2005 Gleneagles Summit represents the most notable site of interaction between the G7/8 and what was then called the 'Outreach Five', which included Brazil, China, India, Mexico, and South Africa. The outreach process, however, followed a model of targeted yet restricted engagement between the incumbent members and the outreach group. BRICS members themselves constituted the core of the outreach group with the exception of Mexico, which has been excluded from the BRICS partially as a result of its membership in the Organisation for Economic Co-operation and Development (OECD). In terms of internal group dynamics, the outreach process facilitated interaction and group cohesion among the BRICS countries (although Russia was separated from them by its membership in the G8), providing them with experience in summitry processes and a shared sense of continued exclusion from and second-class status in the central forums of global governance dominated by the major Western powers.

While the outreach process helped build a sense of cohesion among the BRICS countries themselves, the 2008 global financial crisis catalysed the formation of a BRICS process with a distinctive institutional personality. As with other informal summit processes, including the recalibrated G20, the BRICS did not immediately appear in its final form. Rather, the forum took shape over several incremental stages, with a number of meetings at the foreign ministers' level and an unofficial summit after the 2008 G8 in Toyako, Japan, before being officially elevated to the level of a summit of leaders at Yekaterinburg, Russia, in June 2009.

If cautiously constructed, however, the transition of the BRICS from concept to operational practice marks a major transition in relations between the West and non-West. Up to the creation of the BRICS, the global South acted as a weak demandeur with respect to reform of international institutions. The global financial crisis reversed this relationship. Unlike the Asian financial crisis of the late 1990s, the epicentre of the global financial crisis was not located in the global South, radiating out with worries about a contagion effect spreading to the West. The shocks caused by the 'made in the US' character of the global financial crisis and then the subsequent euro crisis added to the legacy of grievance in the BRICS, but there was now a new-found sense of confidence. Instead of advocating for reforms on normative grounds about fairness, the BRICS based its push on the revised upward movement thanks to its members' competitive performance in the global institutional architecture.

On the one hand, the creation of a new, more inclusive G summit process, with the enlargement from the G7/8 to the G20, has allowed the BRICS to play the role of pivotal insiders in the post-global financial crisis years. The move to incorporate the BRICS into the G20 as the premier forum for economic global governance was quick and seamless, without lengthy and contentious negotiations about the terms of this new relationship. On the other hand, the extension of the BRICS' own stand-alone summit allowed its members to continue to represent themselves as outsiders, preserving their reputation as states opposing the traditional predominance of the West within the global system. This dual status has allowed the BRICS to draw attention to its increasing economic and political weight, while at the same time maintaining members' links to the rest of the global South that have been left out of the key new informal bodies.

The most distinctive feature common to both the established G7/8 and the innovative G20 and the BRICS is the atmosphere of spectacle associated with the summits. This component has magnified both the insider and outsider aspects of the BRICS' personality. The leaders have been given pride of place at some G20 summits, with Brazil's Lula and China's Hu Jintao sitting on either side of George W. Bush at the initial Washington Summit in November 2008. While integrated into the G20 process, however, the BRICS countries have not gained a sense of ownership in the G20 and did not host the initial summits. In addition, the BRICS' sense of exclusivity was diluted by the presence of a number of other countries within the G20 including Mexico, Saudi Arabia, Indonesia, Korea, Argentina, Australia, and Turkey.

The stand-alone summit process, in contrast, signals the complete control of the BRICS countries, and these summits have become

Table 1 BRICS summits, 2008–15

Date	Location
BRIC: 8 July 2008 (unofficial summit)	Toyako, Japan
BRIC: 16 June 2009	Yekaterinburg, Russia
BRIC: 15 April 2010	Brasilia, Brazil
BRICS: 14 April 2011	Sanya, China
BRICS: 29 March 2012	New Delhi, India
BRICS: 26–7 March 2013	Durban, South Africa
BRICS: 15–17 July 2014	Fortaleza, Brazil
BRICS: 8–9 July 2015	Ufa, Russia

the distinctive public face of the BRICS. Held in rotation among the members along the same lines as other informal meetings of the G7/8 and G20, as listed in Table 1, these sites of interaction have allowed the club culture to consolidate within the BRICS.

While the BRICS summits have grown increasingly visible to policy professionals and casual observers alike, questions remain about the underlying logic of the group itself, as well as the motivations of the participating countries. For example, is the move to translate Goldman Sachs' concept to operational reality simply a means to establish a platform signalling the quantitative gaps in economic performance between the BRICS and other entities in the global South? Or, alternatively, is it a mechanism designed to bridge barriers among the BRICS members themselves? Not only has intra-BRICS trade been traditionally low (only some $27 billion in 2002), but major barriers in terms of the movements of people remain. South Africans, for example, enjoy visa-free entry only into Brazil among the five BRICS countries. South Africa, for its part, imposed new visa regulations in May 2014 (with the need for individuals to appear in person for the capture of biometric data), a move that was especially problematic with respect to China because of the existence of visa facilitation centres only in Beijing and Shanghai.

Still, the reason for the intense interest in the trajectory of the BRICS goes well beyond these technical questions. Rather, the sustained interest in the BRICS both within and outside the scholarly community stems from the group's alternative identity as a champion—and an animator—of a shift towards a more multipolar world. In this context, the rise of the BRICS—both the countries themselves and the institutional process associated with the group—signals the emergence of a more diverse international system animated by powers outside the traditional Western establishment. From this perspective, the image of massive size and growth associated with the economic-focused framing device of Goldman Sachs and indeed the alternative framing with respect to a consolidation of a club culture in a summit process are cementing a power transition from the West to a set of more diverse actors.

The declaration of Brazilian president Lula, host of the second official BRICS summit in 2010, that 'a new global economic geography has been born' opens up the questioning even further. Who or what does the BRICS represent? In particular, does the group reflect the narrow interests and the identities of its members or some wider constituency? As noted, the emergence of the BRICS summit represents a departure from the diplomatic practices traditionally embraced by countries of the global South, which emphasize equality, fairness, and solidarity. The BRICS process, in contrast, replaces the notions of solidarity and universality with the promotion of the national interests of a small cluster of emerging market countries that are eager for recognition of their enhanced status both in the West and in the global South. This shift, however, does not necessarily mean that the relationship between the BRICS and the earlier challenge of the global South or 'Third World' has been entirely severed. Although the diplomatic practices of the BRICS countries have shifted significantly, the sense of grievance and status deprivation associated with an earlier era continues to influence them.

Framing the BRICS as a diplomatic project necessitates a closer look at the group's dynamics. At odds with the impression of artificiality because of the role by Goldman Sachs in the creation of the original label, some kind of BRICS-like formation would have appeared on the international stage as a result of the shocks of the global financial crisis and the operational culture of trust built up during the outreach process with the G8. Notwithstanding the structural obstacles in the way of sustainability, the agency of the BRICS countries made sure the forum worked by using informal club mechanisms of cooperation, in the absence of a set physical site, a constitution, a charter, or a fixed schedule. Still, despite the successful establishment and maintenance of the BRICS group, the process is not yet fully formed. The relationship between the BRICS and the G20, for example, remains unclear. The BRICS summit could become a lobby or caucus group within the larger mix of international institutions. Alternatively, the BRICS could increasingly act as a parallel forum, facilitating actions by member states that bypass institutions such as the G20, International Monetary Fund (IMF), or World Bank altogether.

More generally, questions remain about the future of the BRICS as an institution. Will there be enough mortar to keep the BRICS members together? The initial stages of BRICS cooperation were driven largely by external forces that emphasized the reforms that BRICS countries wished to see in the international institutional system. In particular, early cooperation focused heavily on reforming the IMF and the World Bank. Since the 2012 New Delhi Summit, by way of contrast, the focus has turned inward with an initiative designed to establish a South–South development bank independent of the existing 'hub' institutions located in the West. Given the importance of this activity, some detailed analysis is required with respect to the NDB and its

2. The BRICS logo of the 2015 Ufa Summit.

implications for the future of the BRICS. At one level, the ability of BRICS members to mobilize collectively in this fashion offers a test of how ingrained the club culture has become. At another level, the NDB provides indicators of whether the BRICS is able to forge new institutionally-driven links with the rest of the global South, or whether the NDB has become a new source of division, with the NDB being viewed by the rest as a way for BRICS members to pursue their own interests.

The extent to which the BRICS is a state-centric project merits examination as well. The spectacle of summits at the leaders' level remains the most visible feature, with the images of these meetings (as with the logo of the 2015 Ufa Summit in Figure 2) grabbing extensive media coverage.

Yet, underneath this prominent public profile of the summits, there are signs that the BRICS process is beginning to make space available not only for various state officials, but also for non-state actors. Some think tanks and academic centres have gained access to the summit process, although engagement with broader networks remains limited. Conversely, the BRICS process appears to have begun to generate the type of oppositional backlash from certain civil society groups that has long characterized the G7/8 and G20.

Finally, the question of whether the BRICS is a closed or open institution in terms of membership is salient in terms of club culture. South Africa—with strong Chinese backing—was able officially to break into the group in 2010 (with physical attendance at the 2011 Sanya Summit), reconfiguring the original BRIC grouping into the BRICS. More recent institutional developments, particularly the creation of the NDB, point to the potential for further enlargement. Future expansion could take the form of the creation of a 'BRICS-plus' initiative that includes a group of outsider countries as full participants. Alternatively, the forum could seek to add members on a one-off, ad hoc basis.

The lens of club culture may offer valuable views of the current mode of operation, but it is possible that this perspective misses the future path of the BRICS. Moving the debate from focusing on how the BRICS engages the global system as it exists to considering what members would prefer, opens up a different set of questions about the group's role in the global system.

It is difficult for any group that includes both China and Russia to remain impervious to speculation about the possibility, if not the inevitably, of not only an economic challenge but a security one. In earlier eras, the rise of new emerging powers has been marked by geostrategic as well as economic conflict. Can the rise of the BRICS be different? While it remains too early to gauge the true orientation of the group, increasing tensions with the West are evident. In addition, there are signs that the BRICS summitry process itself is being drawn deeper into controversies beyond an exclusively economic agenda. The political character of the BRICS directed towards opposition to the West has recently shifted from externally related concerns, such as those involving Iran, Syria, and Libya, to issues relating to the members themselves. In particular, the situation in Crimea and Ukraine, in which Russia is a pivotal actor, has increased both the salience of the BRICS forum and the intensity of the group's conflict with the West.

Despite adopting an official position of neutrality on the conflict in Ukraine, and refusing to participate in efforts to isolate Russia, the BRICS continues to lack enough internal cohesion or demonstrated ability to undertake the collective action necessary to be termed an alliance. The BRICS cannot be compared to the G7, rooted in clear common interests and shared underlying values, never mind a deep and long-standing institution such as the North Atlantic Treaty Organization. The group's most impressive feature so far has not been a sizeable increase in intra-BRICS trade nor the broadening of a geopolitical projection towards what Russian president Vladimir Putin has termed 'a full-scale strategic management system', but rather its ability both to come into being and to sustain its existence as a forum outside of the West over a substantial period.

Even if the BRICS does not explicitly challenge the traditional Western establishment, it possesses the ability to complicate the workings of the global system dramatically. This potential informs the view of many Western commentators that the BRICS' enhanced role is detrimental to orderly rule making. Simply by possessing some degree of countervailing power—whether underpinned by an alternative vision of world order or not—the BRICS makes policymaking more contentious and time consuming.

Reviewing the three frameworks

In summary, the BRICS can be viewed according to at least three different frameworks. First, as initially conceived by Goldman Sachs, the BRICS is shorthand to describe a set of big and fast-growing economies. Second, the BRICS has developed into an informal diplomatic club with a dual personality as both an insider and outsider in the global system. The BRICS club identity highlights the self-selected nature of the association and the overarching concern of its members with institutional maintenance and survival, not only in moments of ascendancy during the 2008 global financial crisis but also under conditions of stress and fragility. Third, the BRICS can be viewed as representing a geostrategic challenge and possible transformative threat to the existing international order dominated by the United States and the advanced industrial economies of the West. This frame remains more speculative, speaking to the potential for the BRICS to act as a rival to the G7 and a destabilizing force in the Western-centred global system.

Although distinct, these different narratives are interrelated. If the image of economic dynamism is reduced, for example, the BRICS could move towards a more confrontational geostrategic stance. Alternatively, pressure from some members to shift the group towards a more rigid form of oppositional 'bloc' politics could strain the group's informal club culture and threaten its institutional success. Thus, while each framework offers insight into a particular aspect of the BRICS, together they intersect in complex and occasionally contradictory ways. Unlike the collection of studies concerning other institutions, especially the formalized pillars of the post-1945 institutional order (the UN and the IFIs) or the post-1989 post-Cold War era (with a transition from the General Agreement on Tariffs and Trade to the World Trade Organization, WTO), the debates about the BRICS are fresh and intriguing, without the baggage of a voluminous and rather tired bundle of interpretations. Although the historical context of the BRICS remains crucial, the animating motivations and dynamics reflect the state of play in the global rules of the game now and project towards the future.

Chapter 2
A contested invention

Success has many parents, but failure is an orphan. This saying has particular relevance for the rise of the BRICS, as a number of contenders have stepped forward as putative inventors of the term. What began as a device for signifying emerging trends in the global economy has morphed into a political and diplomatic project with important implications for the broader international system.

Although the term has evolved far beyond its roots, credit for the original creation of the BRIC acronym is generally given to Goldman Sachs, and Jim O'Neill in particular through his publication in 2001 of 'Building Better Global Economic BRICs'. The term developed an influence and staying power that other alternatives—labels that cover the spectrum from the Big Ten, MINT, CIVETS, N11, or MIST—have not been able to match. Nevertheless, the creation of the BRIC—and later, with the inclusion of South Africa, the BRICS—did not stem only from the ideas put forward by Goldman Sachs. Even in the absence of an attractive nomenclature, the dynamic of collective action by this cluster of countries held some considerable logic at a time of shifting power dynamics among states.

Concrete diplomatic practice—both in terms of internal and external dynamics—also played an important role in building the

BRICS. The G7/8 outreach process, which brought together Brazil, India, China, Mexico, and South Africa into a group that became known as the 'Outreach Five' (O5), included all the BRICS countries at the table and introduced them to the dynamics of informal 'club' institutions such as the G7/8. Rather than gradually integrating the O5 into the G7/8, however, the outreach process consolidated a shared club culture and sense of like-mindedness among the BRICS countries. Finding themselves deprived of the prospect of equal status through the G7/8, they sought redress in a format of small-group solidarity of their own. This dynamic was facilitated by a number of earlier initiatives and forms of cooperation among subsets of countries within the BRICS, including the creation of the IBSA (India–Brazil–South Africa) Dialogue Forum, the Russia–India–China (RIC) ministerial triangle, and spillover from the Shanghai Cooperation Organization (SCO). In this broader context, the BRIC or BRICS groups are not merely a creation of Goldman Sachs. Rather, the five countries themselves played an important role in transforming the BRICS from a purely analytical device into diplomatic and institutional practice.

Naming the BRIC

Jim O'Neill has given a number of accounts of his invention of the original BRIC label in 2001. Under pressure as the newly appointed head of global economics research at Goldman Sachs to come up with the next big idea on world markets, he looked closely at the non-Western world and found that four countries—Brazil, Russia, India, and China—were responding in the post-Cold War, post-9/11 global environment not by distancing themselves from but by embracing elements of globalization and integration with the core advanced economies.

O'Neill's major breakthrough came through a recognition that these countries on an individual basis were so big, in terms of demographics and economic growth rates, that they possessed sufficient leverage to reshape the world. However, not only

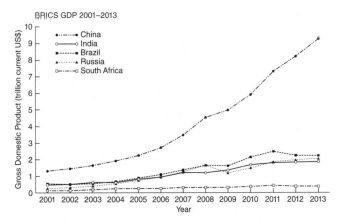

BRICS GDP 2001–2013

Gross Domestic Product (trillion current US$)

• China
○ India
■ Brazil
▲ Russia
□ South Africa

3. BRICS gross domestic product, 2001–13.

the strengths but also the gaps in this framing stood out from the beginning. As an acronym, BRIC had a contrived feel, accentuated by the order of the countries in the acronym. In its use as a marketing tool for selling new markets (including a large spillover of targeted mutual funds such as Schroder International Selection Fund BRIC), BRIC sounded much better than the other possibility—CRIBs—although this listing would have placed China at the beginning where objective criteria suggested it should be (see Figure 3).

Moreover, Russia's outlier status was immediately apparent to a number of observers. While China, India, and Brazil could be authentically categorized as emerging countries—even though with their rich civilizational histories China and India are better cast as re-emerging countries—Russia does not fit this mould. On several counts Russia remains atypical with respect to the other original BRIC members. On the one hand, it maintains some legacy as a great power, with its status as a member of the Permanent Five along with the United States, the United Kingdom, France, and China on the UNSC, and its integration into the G7/8. At the same time, in many ways Russia can be viewed as a declining rather than a rising state. Geostrategically, Russia's territory was fragmented by the collapse of the Soviet Union, while economically, the country's export profile is far more restricted than the other BRIC countries.

Despite these flaws in substantive appraisal, BRIC caught on as a catchy label that depicted the essence of a massive historical transformation. Good timing certainly played a part. The idea of a big cluster of growing, emerging economies was well placed to grab attention in a time of growing anxiety in the West in the aftermath of 9/11 and amid the increasingly uncertain contours of economic globalization. In the November 2001 Goldman Sachs' Global Economic Paper No. 66, 'Building Better Global Economic BRICs', O'Neill grabbed the scope and intensity of the challenge from what he termed the 'emerging giants' that were speeding into the fast lane of the global economy. Through analysis and comparison of growth forecasts, he identified the four original BRIC countries as capable of overtaking the G7 countries in their economic capabilities by 2050. Two years later, Goldman Sachs embellished on these themes opened up by O'Neill. This extended analysis predicted that the BRIC would overtake the incumbents of the old establishment at a faster rate than previously forecasted. In terms of scope of impact, it highlighted the importance of considering the ranking of the BRIC in terms of GDP based on PPP: with China (second), India (fourth), Russia (sixth), and Brazil (ninth)—all in the top ten of the global league tables.

None of this extended exploration was entirely novel. China's economic rise extended back to its agricultural reforms of the mid-1970s, supplemented in the 1990s with large increases of foreign direct investment (FDI) in manufacturing. The average growth rate in China since the late 1970s stood at approximately 9.4 per cent, with only two years' growth below 5 per cent, in 1989 and 1990. In India, major policy reforms started in the late 1980s triggered a higher rate of growth, albeit slower than in China, with sustained GDP growth of 4 per cent to 6 per cent annually over a span of twenty years. Furthermore, notwithstanding the emphasis of Goldman Sachs on the parallel paths of the BRIC members, the contrasts are as important, with growth in India being led by the services sector rather than exports of manufactures financed by FDI inflows, as in China.

The problems with including Russia in the mix have grown more pronounced. The Russian case differs sharply from the other BRIC countries, with a sharply negative growth in the immediate post-Soviet period. The main reason for Russia's economic recovery was the sharp devaluation of ruble in 1998. Growth after that transition period exceeded 7 per cent annually, driven by energy exports (oil and gas), especially during the period of high world oil prices before the sharp declines through 2014 and 2015.

Brazil enjoyed strong growth at approximately 7 per cent annually from 1940 until the debt crises of the 1980s. This period was followed with moves towards a more open economy and privatization. Strong growth returned in the mid-1990s, but was halted by the end of the decade with yet another currency crisis. Economic growth in Brazil continues to be volatile, although export growth in agriculture and natural resources as well as a fairly young population are impressive strengths.

The Goldman Sachs publications presented an optimistic perspective of the BRIC countries in a manner that captured the popular imagination of investors and the wider public. The common attributes of a positive nature were showcased: large populations with a rapid increase of urban dwellers, low wage rates, episodes of sustained high growth, growing inflows and outflows of FDI, high rates of growth of trade and, consequently, fast accumulation of foreign exchange reserves, and growing domestic demand as a result of increased individual incomes and overall economic development.

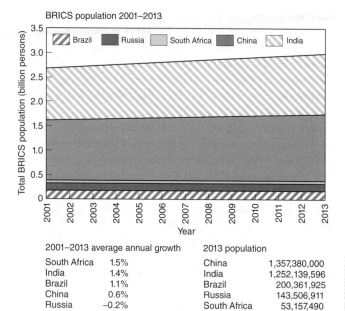

4. BRICS population 2001–13.

By contrast, the features that acted as brakes instead of motors
driving developmental progress were downplayed by Goldman
Sachs. Population dynamics (see Figure 4) provide sources of
weakness as well as strength. China is at great risk of becoming
old before it becomes rich. India's high population growth will make
this country the largest in the world within the next two decades,
but will also bring increased tensions over the distribution of
resources. Russia is struggling with sizeable population shrinkage.
Other factors that act as brakes—including high levels of pollution
and corruption—also cannot be ignored.

The gaps in analysis were exacerbated by the reluctance of
Goldman Sachs to tease out the implications of the rise of the
BRIC for the current, US-dominated global order. O'Neill, to his
credit, mused about the BRIC's impact on institutional reform.

But it was the pattern of growth itself, not the political ramifications, that remained the main game. In the short term, his strategic approach embellished the importance of the original grouping, with China, India, Russia, and Brazil. In the longer term he signalled the advent of a BRIC-plus world, with other concentric rings of countries inclusive of the N11 and MIST added to the original core.

Goldman Sachs is commonly associated with the concept of decoupling, a process by which components of the global economy are disconnected. A Goldman Sachs Economic Research paper in 2007 predicted for example that 'China, together with emerging Asia, stands a very good chance of decoupling from the US economy in the coming few years'. Nonetheless, O'Neill constantly questioned whether this was an accurate assessment. While highlighting the fact that global demand was higher in China and the other BRICS than in the US amid the shocks of the financial crisis, he nuanced his argument by pointing out that global markets had not decoupled.

Deficiencies in the established club format

The private sector's recognition of the original BRIC members as important fast-growing economies in an increasingly interdependent world had its benefits. This preparatory work eased the way for legitimizing the group as it moved from a virtual existence to reality. Still, while pointing towards the logic of a BRIC group in practice, Goldman Sachs did not map out the path towards collective action.

The rationale for recognizing enhanced membership status was based on the perception that the institutional status quo was not adequate either symbolically or instrumentally for dealing with the circumstances of the 21st century. This perception was particularly acute with regard to the G8, as it was regarded even by some of its leading members as suffering from an enormous legitimacy gap because of its restricted Western-centric membership. In 2003, Jacques Chirac of France became the first Western leader to announce that the G8 was no longer inclusive enough. Accordingly, he invited the leaders of several countries beyond the West, including Brazil and India, to attend the Evian Summit.

British Prime Minister Tony Blair followed up in a similar vein, inviting a group of outreach countries that included China, India, Brazil, and South Africa to the Gleneagles Summit in 2005. The functional rationale for inviting these countries, and not others, stemmed from a recognition that they were responsible for high greenhouse gas emissions and were therefore vital to climate change and energy negotiations. The composition of the O5 was, in turn, institutionalized two years later when German chancellor Angela Merkel invited its members to join the so-called Heiligendamm Process in 2007, a mechanism intended to promote dialogue and cooperation between G8 and O5 officials on specific issues.

From an incumbent G8 perspective, this mode of accommodating major countries beyond the West was deemed a success, even though differences persisted about whether it marked the beginning or the end of the exercise. Germany, Japan, and Canada had very little appetite for any G8 expansion. Even so, they supported the idea of a dialogue between the G8 and the O5, and of creating a secretariat within the OECD—the classic 'rich' Western club, although one that also embraced outreach with the emerging powers—to manage informally the relationship between the old and new establishment. President Nicolas Sarkozy of France, in contrast, advocated integrating the two groupings even further. As he argued in one speech: 'The G8 can't meet for two days and the G13 [the G8 plus the O5] for just two hours. That doesn't seem fitting, given the power of these five emerging countries.'

However, the O5 members, each connected to the global South, perceived their relationship with the G8 Heiligendamm Process not as a breakthrough, but rather as a constraint on their ascendancy.

When the outreach was stripped to its bare essentials, China, India, Brazil, and South Africa were reluctant to embrace a model that sharply differentiated between the status of the old establishment and the aspirations of the new. Although they were willing to engage in the process, even on an asymmetrical basis, the countries refused to engage in concrete negotiations. Thus, rather than working towards real deliverables, the big non-Western states took advantage of the initiative to reinforce their internal collaboration.

This collaboration began below the leaders' level. The sherpas—state officials who do the preparatory heavy lifting on behalf of the leaders—for the O5 countries consulted with each other in separate meetings from those of the G8. A distinct culture of a caucus meeting developed among the leaders on the sidelines of the G8 summit. Meetings held before the G8 were designed to coordinate policies, supplemented by joint press conferences to disseminate responses to the discussion, such as the one held by the O5 leaders in Sapporo on their way to the Toyako Summit in 2008. Moreover, although not well publicized at the time, in Toyako Russian President Dmitry Medvedev, Chinese President Hu Jintao, Indian Prime Minister Manmohan Singh, and Brazilian President Luiz Inácio Lula da Silva held a meeting. Indeed, for some analysts (especially those in Russia) this meeting constitutes the first BRIC summit, at which the foreign ministers of the four countries were instructed to follow up in order to coordinate approaches on key economic issues.

In a significant symbolic display (as shown in Figure 5) of the level of solidarity reached by the O5, in 2009 Lula handed out Brazilian football shirts with the number five at the L'Aquila Summit as a display of apartness from the G8.

Several mishaps with respect to the Heiligendamm Process closed the door to this option of gradually reforming the G8. The most infamous incident was the release of the communiqué that

5. **Outreach Five leaders at the 2009 G8 L'Aquila Summit. Brazilian President Luiz Inácio Lula da Silva presents his fellow Outreach Five leaders with T-shirts signed by the Brazilian football team at the 2009 L'Aquila Summit. From left to right: Manmohan Singh of India, Felipe Calderón of Mexico, Lula, Jacob Zuma of South Africa, and Dai Bingguo, the state councillor who replaced China's President Hu Jintao who left suddenly because of the July 2009 Ürümqi riots between Uyghurs and Han-Chinese.**

announced the establishment of the Heiligendamm Process without any input from the O5 and before the outreach countries actually joined the G8 meetings. Manmohan Singh's remark—'We have come here not as petitioners but as partners in an equitable, just and fair management of the global comity of nations which we accept as the reality in the globalized world'—reinforced a hopeful statement from China that the G8 outreach would not be used as 'a means of exerting pressure on developing countries'.

On the O5 side, the G8 simply had too much baggage. China traditionally focused on formal, more inclusive structures, above all the UN, but with enhanced involvement in the IMF and entry into the WTO in December 2001. It never actively sought full membership in the G8. Although comfortable with the language of dialogue, cooperation, and partnership, it had serious reservations about a tight embrace. In addition to protecting its developing-country status, China was wary of full membership and wanted to avoid any attempts at 'socialization' by the Western powers and any possible pressure on domestic policies, to which Beijing is very sensitive.

For India and Brazil, potential entry into the G8 was never as important as gaining permanent membership in the UNSC. Enlargement of the G8 would be something of a consolation prize (and a stepping stone) after the failed campaigns aimed at Security Council reform that foundered at the largely disappointing UN World Summit in 2005. Both these countries have a very strong self-image rooted in the developing world. Akin to China, both expected more recognition of their growing global role and pushed for comprehensive reforms in the established governance architecture.

South Africa in the post-apartheid years after 1994 was thrust, awkwardly, into representing the 'African voice' on the global stage. It was embraced as the ideal partner in Africa for the G8, despite strong reservations throughout the continent to such a designation. As much as South Africa strongly supported the O5 and the Heiligendamm Process as structured opportunities for expanding the dialogue, it saw them as only one element for improving the wider relationship of Africa with the West. A major challenge for South Africa's diplomacy was how to navigate the dialogue with the G8 so as not to be accused of 'selling out' by other African countries and so improve its legitimacy on the continent.

Only Mexico hung on to the value of the O5 process as more than a means to an end. Mexico chaired the O5 and hosted the first meeting of its steering committee in January 2010. For the other participants, nonetheless, the O5–G8 dialogue had run its course. By the Italian L'Aquila 2009 Summit, the O5—as evidenced by

Lula's football shirts—had consolidated a collective personality not only as the necessary core partners of the G8 but also as the essential ingredients in any institutional reform process.

If a failure in terms of its initial purpose, the O5 was the perfect complement to the Goldman Sachs project of identification. To the parallelism of economic trajectory was now added the catalyst of frustrated ambitions. The majority of O5 countries construed what the G8 considered to be a form of generous engagement as too little too late. The awkwardness of the G8–O5 process worked as a barrier, not a bridge. The rising states were willing to be brought into an updated concert of powers via an elevated G20, but the outreach experience convinced them to rethink their own autonomous approach in the global system.

Precursors to the BRICS forum

If the concept of the BRICs emerged from market-driven intellectual inspiration, cooperation among the BRICS states was not unprecedented. Consistent with the diversity of the group with respect to history, size, economic profile, and political systems, each country brought—and continues to bring—a particular set of national preferences to the ongoing creation of the BRICS process and the various forms of cooperation that preceded it. For China in particular—the largest and most economically powerful member—the forum represented a means to expand the country's influence in a cautious manner, thus allowing it to lead the process 'from behind'.

One indication of how China initially remained on the sidelines was its absence from IBSA, a process that was initiated in conjunction with the G8's outreach. South African president Thabo Mbeki proposed a subgroup ahead of the June 2003 Evian Summit, to which these three countries had been invited by French President Jacques Chirac. Soon after, the three countries signed a declaration to create IBSA when the foreign ministers of

India, Brazil, and South Africa met in Brasilia at the first IBSA Dialogue Forum. This forum laid the foundations for a number of low key, but nevertheless significant, initiatives among the three countries and their respective regions as epitomized by MERCOSUR (Mercado Común del Sur, or the Common Market of the South) and the Southern African Development Community (SADC)—although not the South Asian Association for Regional Cooperation (SAARC) in the case of India.

One outcome was the strengthening of business-to-business links via the IBSA Business Council. In addition, IBSA spawned a series of activities linking non-state actors to the initiative, including a Women's Forum. All of these components played up the like-minded, 'vibrant democratic' components of the IBSA connection, with a focus on the competitive advantages of the Indian–Brazilian–South African private sector and robust civil society.

Another sign of China's preference to lead from behind was revealed with respect to the separate RIC strategic trilateral channel. Despite China's economic and political weight, Russia has taken the lead within the trilateral relationship. This alternative informal grouping emphasized, far more explicitly than the O5 and IBSA, differentiation from the West rather than engagement with it. Members expressed solidarity with the US vis-à-vis the terrorist attacks of 9/11, an attitude enhanced by Russia's concern over Chechnya—sentiments that were echoed by China's worries over Muslim militants in Xinjiang province, and India's anxiety over Kashmir. But the overarching themes in the RIC focused on advancing towards a multipolar world.

At first glance, then, it is the differences not the similarities that jump out between IBSA and RIC. The democratic ethos of IBSA meshed with the aspirations of Brazil and India (and, in the background, South Africa) to permanent UNSC membership. There was also a strong normative component. The initiative thus connected with several ongoing issue-oriented campaigns, such as the joint effort to move beyond the regime of patent control of HIV/AIDS drugs and to provide generic drugs to domestic patients. It nudged the IBSA countries to move into new terrain, such as taking on the coordination role in three projects financed by the United Nations Development Programme: the first in Haiti concerning waste management, a second in Guinea-Bissau on agricultural development, and the third in Cape Verde with a healthcare clinic.

In symbolic terms the great benefit of building on IBSA's strengths was to tap into the soft power attributes of the three countries. This capacity was epitomized by the charismatic personality of Lula, who assumed office on 1 January 2003. Playing to Brazil's identity as a rising global power, albeit one firmly rooted in its geographic location in South America and as leader of the global South, Lula raised his personal profile on the international stage through the combination of extensive travelling and a willingness to raise his voice on pivotal global issues.

The real impact of Brazilian diplomacy shone through when directed at trade issues at a decisive moment via the 2003 WTO ministerial meeting in Cancún. With Russia still not a member and China playing a low-key role after its accession in 2001, Brazil mobilized a strong coalition to block any attempt by the old establishment to cut a deal that could be imposed across the board. Brazil's frustrations surfaced especially on the unwillingness of the United States and the European Union to cut agricultural subsidies. On top of instrumental self-interest, though, Brazil wanted to punctuate the point that the global South would no longer concede to the incumbents dictating the institutional rules of the game.

While the position of the RICs was not in sync with IBSA on a range of issues, there was enough common interest to build a more comprehensive informal grouping. On the one hand, IBSA demonstrated a willingness to move into the geostrategic sphere, as exhibited by the IBSAMAR (India–Brazil–South Africa Maritime) exercise. In 2008, 2010, and 2014, the three countries conducted anti-air, anti-submarine warfare, and anti-piracy drills. On the other hand, Russia expanded its vision beyond RIC to bring Brazil into a more elaborate initiative through a process of 'multifaceted quadripartite cooperation'. The IBSA and RIC processes—coupled with the G8 outreach experience—thus served as crucial precursors to the emergence of the BRICS as a diplomatic phenomenon.

Building a forum of their own

Building on the growing experience of cooperation among the members, the BRICS (or more precisely BRIC prior to South Africa joining in 2010) began to take shape incrementally in the years prior to the 2008 global financial crisis. The process can be traced to September 2006, when the BRIC foreign ministers assembled on the side of the sixty-first UN General Assembly in New York. This initial meeting possessed the type of low-key character evident in other gatherings among BRIC officials before the financial crisis. The first meeting at the leaders' level was an unofficial one at the end of the G8 summit in Toyako in July 2008, and they tasked their foreign ministers with setting the date for their first official summit. The second and third meetings of the BRIC foreign ministers took place in Russia, while annual meetings at the level of deputy foreign ministers were also quietly established. Over the same period, regular contacts began to be established among embassies and permanent representatives of the BRIC countries at key sites of multilateral diplomacy.

If the building blocks were in place for the launch of a stand-alone forum prior to 2009, however, a jolt was still required for the process to be elevated to a summit at the leaders' level. The

catalytic moment came with the global financial crisis.
As highlighted by the creation of the elevated G20 summit in
November 2008, the circumstances of these shocks were
especially conducive to bold types of institutional innovation.
Similar to the G20, the institutional personality of the BRIC
and subsequently BRICS did not need to be invented from scratch
in the scramble to react to the stress of new circumstances.
All the ingredients were in place. There just needed to be a
decisive push.

The ideas first put forward by Goldman Sachs—predicated on the
rise of a group of large emerging economies and the resulting
transformation of the global economy—were given added weight
by the financial crisis. While the crisis, centred in the United
States, dealt a blow to the economic and normative power of the
West, the BRIC countries appeared poised to survive and even
thrive as the crisis unfolded. In a media commentary prior to the
first summit of leaders, Lula pointed out the mix of statistics that
were at the heart of the Goldman Sachs analysis: 'We stand out
because in recent years our four economies have shown robust
growth...we now generate 65 per cent of world growth, which
makes us the main hope for a swift recovery from global
recession.'

The reverberations of the global financial crisis thus acted as
catalysts that elevated and solidified pre-existing structures of
cooperation. Backed by their leaders, the BRIC foreign ministers
pushed forward with coordination on key economic issues. Such a
focus in turn led to meetings of finance ministers and central bank
governors. But with both the shift within the G20 as well as the
experience of the sideline meeting at Toyako as models, the focal
point for cooperation among the BRIC countries quickly rose to
the leaders' level. Announced in late November 2008, by Russian
President Dmitry Medvedev during a visit to Brazil, the first
official summit of the BRIC leaders took place in Yekaterinburg,
Russia, in mid-June 2009.

Moving to the next stage of institutional development

Although prompted by the destabilizing impact of the global financial crisis, cooperation among the BRIC/BRICS members emerged from deeper historical and ideational roots. While the label itself was coined as BRIC by a New York-based investment bank, cooperation among the countries themselves stemmed to a large extent from a sense of collective grievance and frustration at the behaviour of the old Western establishment. The decision by this group of countries to establish a diplomatic club of their own can be tied both to their rising economic and political weight, as well as to a shared sense that their elevated status was not adequately reflected in existing international institutions dominated by developed states.

In this context, the global financial crisis brought to the fore the fundamental predicament of the BRIC/BRICS relationship with the G7/8. Instrumentally, amid the shocks, there was a clearer appreciation by the G8 members that they could not deal with the global financial crisis alone. In the face of diminished economic and normative power, the G8 recognized it needed to bring rising powers to the table. Yet, at the same time, obstacles to full and equal cooperation between the two groups—both symbolic and substantive—persisted. The old Western establishment controlled the hosting and agenda of the first four G20 summits. In addition, by broadening out the membership to allies—Korea, Indonesia, Australia, Turkey, and Saudi Arabia—the United States could be seen as acting to dilute the BRIC members' influence as rising powers.

Under these conditions, the BRIC's ambivalence towards the G20 was understandable. Because of status aspirations and the need to tackle the significant concerns raised by the financial crisis, none of BRICs wanted to stay on the outside. As participants in the initial G20 summit in Washington DC in November 2008, all the BRIC leaders became willing members of a recalibrated global hierarchy. However, they did not consider this mode of informality to be their exclusive option. Building on the club culture initiated in the O5 process and embellished in the separate paths of IBSA and RIC, they kept their options open in terms of institutional preferences. Hedging their bets, the BRIC countries balanced their membership in the G20 with a summit of their own to increase their prominence.

Chapter 3
A historical departure

As both a diplomatic project and an international institution, the BRICS is fascinating in its mixing of unique and generic practices. Historically, a fundamental objective of rising powers has been to institutionalize their new status. From this perspective the common and persistent demand by the BRICS for institutional reform stretching across formal organizations such as the IFIs, as well as a diminution of established self-selective clubs (such as the OECD) dominated by the West, is predictable. The feelings of grievance and frustration evidenced by the BRICS countries about the biases of the existing international system, as well as their desire to play a magnified role as a result of their growing economic and political clout, echo the sentiments of previous rising states.

In a host of other ways, though, the BRICS challenge marks a complete historical departure. The most common means by which ascendant powers gain new institutional privileges is at the end of a major war as a member of a winning coalition. This scenario was true of the case of Prussia, which became part of the 1814–15 concert of powers after playing an important part in defeating Emperor Napoleon Bonaparte of France. Although complicated by the hold of isolationism in US domestic politics, American president Woodrow Wilson's pivotal role in the 1919 Paris peace process also conformed to this model, in that the United States entered World War I in 1917 on the side of the British–French alliance. And a similar dynamic played out in the ability of the USSR to gain a privileged status as a permanent, veto-wielding member of the Permanent Five of the UNSC through its costly efforts alongside the United States and Britain in defeating Nazi Germany.

The role of the BRICS in terms of its extended pattern of informal institutionalization is completely different. The catalyst for members' new type of engagement—mainly via the G summits and the outreach process—was not because BRICS countries had been grouped among the winners in a decisive security-related rupture in the global system. On the contrary, in ideological if not in explicit military terms, two members can be said to have 'lost' the Cold War. Yet, rather than being isolated and punished, some momentum built up for Russia and China, along with non-aligned India and Brazil, to be brought deeper into the core global institutional architecture after the end of East–West bipolarity.

An acknowledgement of a dual legitimacy–efficiency gap, especially within the activities of the G7/8 summit process, drove this interactive process. Indeed, without the participation of the BRICS, the pattern of global governance looked increasingly incomplete. The growing economic and political weight of the BRICS countries, coupled with the apparent decline of the United States and European countries in the aftermath of the 2008 global financial crisis, raised questions about the appropriateness of existing rules and governance structures and, particularly, about the exclusion of major emerging market economies from core decision-making bodies such as the G7. Not only was the legitimacy deficit highly visible, due to the asymmetry between the position of the traditional Western rule makers and the non-Western rule takers, but the capacity for efficient institutional performance through a more inclusive approach was apparent. In order for the global system to work, the BRICS needed to be accorded a greater pride of place.

Evolving modes of interaction focus increasingly on dealing with complex transnational problems rather than on the dominant concerns of the earlier 19th- and 20th-century concerts of powers, related primarily to the (re)allocation of territory and movements of people along with preventing costly wars among great powers. Cross-border issues in the economic, social, and environmental spheres reveal both a deepening systematic interdependence among states and a clear divergence in national priorities and interests. In this context, the turn towards engagement between the BRICS and the G7 lacked 'like-minded' glue. The members of BRICS were not linked to the West in forms of common geopolitical engagement, nor did they share a vision of what advances in the rules of the global system should look like. This lack of common ground is clearly visible in the security sphere, animated by growing tensions between the BRICS and the West on the ongoing conflicts in Syria and Ukraine. Russia's move at the 2014 Fortaleza and 2015 Ufa Summits to try to gain collective support for its aggressive actions in the Crimea and Ukraine further raised the prospect of the BRICS moving towards a confrontational geostrategic position vis-à-vis the West.

Ongoing differences have thus limited the ability of the BRICS and the G7 to engage on an institutional basis. As a result, the BRICS countries have been motivated to establish a parallel mode of autonomous, informal diplomatic mobilization independent of the G summit processes. Despite increased representation in the expanded G process—including the G20 leaders' forum and the reformed Financial Stability Board—the BRICS does not possess complete 'ownership' of these processes, as evidenced by the failure of any BRICS country to host the G20 before 2013.

Still, the accommodation of the BRICS countries in the G20 likely counteracts any strategy of full opposition and resistance to the established international order. Although the geopolitical differences between the West and the BRICS have ratcheted up, few if any commentators see the BRICS as a cohesive anti-Western alliance. Certainly the declaratory statements used by the BRICS leaders to express their resentment and frustration with the global system, with the emphasis on the requirement for equality in the global system through a shift to multipolarity, are very different from the language used by the main challengers of the past, whether Prussia's aspiration to find its 'place in the sun' or the USSR's openly expressed goal to 'bury' the West during the Cold War.

Any equation of the BRICS in the 21st century to the challenge of the Third World of the 1960s and 1970s also has severe limitations. Although these movements, akin to the BRICS, were driven by underlying power dynamics, they nevertheless stressed the broader solidarity of the global South against the West. The campaign for the New International Economic Order (NIEO), for example, demanded the reduction of international inequalities through various mechanisms such as resource transfers from the North to the South. Although the BRICS countries continue to profess their links and solidarity with other members of the global South, the creation of the BRICS diplomatic process signals the collapse of this older type of solidarity politics. Rather than using an ideology of solidarity via 'Third Worldism', the BRICS exerts a leverage that stems from the growing weight and capacity of its individual members. In contrast to past movements, members are not asserting the need to change the international system to address issues such as poverty and economic inequality. Rather, they are contesting the international order on the basis of their rising economic and political power.

Tempering the differences

To present the BRICS as a unique phenomenon is not to dismiss a number of counterarguments that showcase potential commonalities with the features of past challenges. As with previous challengers, the BRICS must temper members' differences in both political and economic power as well as national interests and preferences. More specifically, the phenomenon shares two overarching features with previous challenges to the international status quo: the presence of a single, dominant, challenging state within the coalition, and the origins of the movement in severe crisis and disruption within the global economy and broader international system. Despite these common features, the BRICS remains unique.

Based on a variety of measures, China is clearly exceptional within the BRICS. Over a range of statistical criteria, it dominates its fellow members. Indeed, a more accurate label for the group as acknowledged by Goldman Sachs is CRIBS, not BRICS, with a big C out in front of the acronym. The model of a developmental state, with a wide-scale presence of state-owned enterprises, has propelled China's spectacular growth in share of GDP average growth rate, and merchandise exports, among many other important measures when compared with the other original BRICs (see Table 2).

Graham Allison, director of Harvard University's Belfer Center for Science and International Affairs, has identified the major difference in scale between the rate of growth of China and the other BRICS members between 2008 and 2013, with China's economy expanding at double the rate of the rest of the members. While China has always been the colossus within the group, this status has become more pronounced. Allison also points out that China in 2013 accounted for double the global merchandise trade of the rest of the BRICS members combined, and held twice the foreign reserves as the others. Allison suggests that China should be disengaged from the remaining countries, which he terms 'RIBS'.

This asymmetrical distribution of capabilities returns the focus of analysis away from the uniqueness of the BRICS to the privileging of an individual country on the rise. The only puzzle lies in how the ascendancy of this single country is to be interpreted. From the

Table 2 BRICS development indicators

Indicator	Brazil	Russia	India	China	South Africa
Population (2013)	200.4 million	143.5 million	1.252 billion	1.357 billion	53.15 million
GDP (US$) (2013)	2.246 trillion	2.097 trillion	1.877 trillion	9.24 trillion	350.6 billion
GDP per capita (US$) (2013)	11,208.08	14,611.70	1,498.87	6,807.43	6,617.91
GDP annual growth rate (%) (2014)	0.1	0.6	7.4	7.4	1.5
GDP average growth rate 2000–14 (%) (2001–15)	3.3	4.6	7.0	9.7	3.2
Merchandise exports	225 billion	496 billion	317 billion	2,342 billion	91 billion
Total reserves (includes gold, current $US)	363 billion	386 billion	325 billion	3,900 billion	49 billion

Compiled from data from the World Bank Development Indicators perspective of an embedded dynamic of complex interdependence, the key relationship is not among the BRICS members but between China and the United States. To capture the salience of this connection, Harvard-based economic historian Niall Ferguson coined the term 'Chimerica' to describe the combination of Chinese overproduction and US overconsumption dominating the world economy. In this context, the BRICS phenomenon can be interpreted as simply disguising China as a sole and singular challenger to the United States in both the security and economic realms.

Nevertheless, any preference for detaching China from the BRICS as a descriptive or analytical device does not detract from the group's relevance as a political and diplomatic project. For China, operating through informal groupings—be it the BRICS or the G20—allows the country to avoid international attention associated with unilateral action on a host of key global issues. This type of engagement reinforces China's impression as a 'responsible stakeholder' in the global system. Indeed, the dominant power within the established system—the United States—has not worked explicitly to contain China's rise. Initially, the nature of this response was in large part due to a deficiency of attention. Whereas Britain and France were acutely aware of the increased power of Prussia, and the United States was aware of the challenge from the Soviet Union in the Cold War years, 9/11 directed American attention away from China towards the Middle East and South Central Asia. Although the Obama administration's 'pivot' towards Asia undoubtedly reflects China's increased clout within the region, the two countries have so far avoided the type of direct oppositional dynamic that has marked relations between established and rising powers.

In its origins, the BRICS phenomenon also bears some similarities to previous coalitions of challenger states. Unlike the examples already discussed—Prussia/Germany, the United States, and the USSR—the BRICS challenge has not emerged directly from war among the great powers. Nonetheless, the catalysts for the origin of this group can be interpreted with some accuracy as a combination of shocks to the global system that occurred during the decade from 2000 to 2010. The terrorist attacks against the World Trade Center and Pentagon on 11 September 2001 represent the first of these shocks, and demonstrated the vulnerability of even the most powerful states in the face of extremism and globalized violence. While the attacks themselves generated widespread sympathy and support for the United States, the events that followed, particularly the Iraq War and the Abu Ghraib prisoner abuse scandal, dealt a blow to its legitimacy and soft power. Finally, the 2008 global financial crisis, which originated in the United States, was a further blow to that country's perceived pre-eminence and, ultimately, catalysed the BRICS challenge.

Those sceptical of the BRICS as a political and diplomatic project view the shift towards informal summitry by its members as a means to disguise a lack of common interests and purpose. In this view, the BRICS represents a distraction with little real impact. Far from a viable instrumental challenge at the apex of power, the BRICS phenomenon is a symbolic exercise, with much media attention but little in the way of action or concrete delivery.

Framed in this fashion, the BRICS appears to have more in common with collective Third World initiatives such as the Non-Aligned Movement (NAM) or the push for an NIEO. The solidarity ethos associated with the Group of 77 (G77) developing countries and the NAM went beyond a single rising state such as the threat of Prussia/Germany or the USSR. These movements stemmed from a collective sense of disaffection with the rules of the game, not because of classic big power rivalry (as exhibited through races to produce the most battleships or launch satellites into space) but because of an overall condition of exclusion and vulnerability. As the anticipatory Bandung Conference of Asian and African states signalled in 1955, the goals of the Third World

6. The Bandung precedent of leaders' summitry. China's Premier Zhou Enlai speaks to his fellow leaders at the conference of Asian and African states in Bandung, Indonesia, in 1955.

movement remained tied to concerns about a lack of consultation by the West, the relationship of a still closed-off China with the rest of the world, and the legacy of colonialism.

Akin to the BRICS countries, the challengers from the global South in the earlier era made use of informal modes of institutionalization. The Bandung Conference featured the presence of Prime Minister Jawaharlal Nehru of India, Presidents Gamal Abdel Nasser of Egypt and Kwame Nkrumah of Ghana, Yugoslavia's Marshal Josip Tito, China's Premier Zhou Enlai (pictured in Figure 6), as well as the host, President Sukarno from Indonesia—thus making effective use of high-profile meetings up to the level of leaders.

Into the 1970s and beyond, by contrast, this cluster of developing countries grew suspicious of this type of diplomatic informality.

This attitude stemmed from attempts by the United States and the West to reinvigorate themselves through new, narrowly constructed forums such as the G7 and the International Energy Agency. Informal practices thus came to be associated with the diplomatic strategies of powerful states and the exclusion of the countries of the global South. In this context, the demand for an NEIO—focused on redistribution and greater equality—was channelled, for the most part, through caucus groups or advocate organizations with some fixed attachment to formal UN institutions, notably the United Nations Conference on Trade and Development.

Still, the global South of the 1960s and 1970s lacked the ability to offer an attractive development model and ultimately the collective effort to establish an NIEO collapsed in the face of sustained opposition from the United States and United Kingdom. Throughout the 1970s and 1980s, the response from the core Western countries was expressed antagonistically, with stigmatization, deflection, and the exploitation of divisions within the global South. The only serious effort to bridge this gap came in 1981 with twenty-three world leaders attending the Meeting on International Cooperation and Development in Cancún, which emerged in the aftermath of the 1980 report 'North-South: A Program for Survival' released by the Brandt Commission that aimed to bridge divisions on global development. Although intellectually promising, however, this overture was blunted by the hard force of the political counter-response led by British prime minister Margaret Thatcher and US president Ronald Reagan throughout the 1980s.

Though there are some similarities, the BRICS' position in the 21st century is distinct from that of the countries of the global South in the 1970s and 1980s. The push for the NIEO was buoyed by rising oil prices and the associated 'producer power' acquired by certain states in the developing world. However, the sustained economic growth of the BRICS countries places them in a position of strength distinct from previous coalitions. Differences in position have translated into shifts in diplomatic practice. In contrast to earlier periods that emphasized solidarity and resistance, the BRICS countries are willing to engage closely with the established powers of the G7. This positioning has gained prominence despite voices in the wider global South that prefer to resist negotiation and accommodation. Indeed, despite maintaining good relations with countries in the oppositional camp, such as Venezuela (led up to 2013 by Hugo Chávez) and members of the Bolivarian Alliance for the Peoples of Our America, this stance does not condition the behaviour of the BRICS forum or its members. In the same mode, while continuing to give declaratory preference to the UN, BRICS members became more entangled in broader informal institutionalization.

This adaptability in dealing with the old Western establishment reflects a readiness to downplay traditional principles that animated previous challenges by coalitions of developing states. In particular, the BRICS countries have willingly abandoned the principles of sovereign equality of states in favour of institutionalized recognition of their new status. The creation of the BRICS, together with the presence of all the BRICS members within the G20, is a far cry from the push for universal participation and a collective 'emancipation' of developing countries. As such, demands for equal treatment for the rest of the global South have been transformed into a sustained campaign for special and differentiated treatment for a select cluster of emerging market countries. This shift marks a departure from traditional modes of cooperation within the global South, and provides an opportunity to enhance developing countries' influence and shape the global agenda.

This process of strategic adaptation has been reflected in procedural flexibility in negotiations. The demands for global redistribution made by the Third World challengers in the 1960s and 1970s were framed as zero-sum. BRICS members, in contrast, have accepted many aspects of the current, Western-centred international system. Of course, the BRICS phenomenon itself has been motivated at least partially by members' ongoing dissatisfaction with the pace of change in existing international institutions. Rather than pushing for a total and immediate transformation, however, the BRICS countries have adopted a more patient and pragmatic approach. Resistance to blocking specific policy initiatives has thus not emerged as part of a larger and more general oppositional approach to the functioning of traditional institutions themselves. Membership in the G20 has moved BRICS members into a different position as insiders in the existing international system. This position stands in sharp contrast therefore to the maximalist outsider demands of the challengers from the global South in the 1960s and 1970s that placed the responsibility for change exclusively on the old establishment from the North.

Moving beyond past models

A review of the history of North–South and South–South relations helps clarify the unique nature of the BRICS. The dynamic of the group, while echoing some specific features from past eras, diverges fundamentally from historical models. Despite some continuity, these elements are overwhelmed by the group's distinctiveness. While the presence of China suggests some commonalities with the experience of previous rising states, the current period has several unique characteristics: the sheer number of new challengers, the lack of dramatic rupture or direct challenge to the foundations of the old system, the maintenance of cooperation in various aspects of global governance, and the lack of a structured confrontation between rising and established powers.

This is not to deny that some sharp, destabilizing turn by the BRICS is possible. Indeed, the BRICS approach could shift to highlight confrontation with the incumbents of the old establishment. Russia—somewhat of an outlier within the BRICS itself—has already begun to take an increasingly oppositional stance to the

West through its push to consolidate its own sphere of influence in a Euraslan Economic Union. The impression of an escalating geostrategic rivalry between the BRICS and the West is further reinforced by China's increased assertiveness in regard to its territorial claims, and the accompanying US 'pivot' to Asia, intended to reassure American allies in the region.

Nevertheless, as yet there is little evidence that the BRICS members are committed to any revisionist collective action that would challenge the fundamental character of the post-1945 international system, and these issues have not yet intruded into the dynamics of the BRICS process itself. Rather, the emphasis so far has been on hedging and institutional maintenance rather than outright opposition and 'hard balancing'. Moreover, while the narrative of multipolarism and democratization of the global system remains strong, initiatives to establish tangible alternatives have continued to be cautious and targeted.

The prime illustration here is the BRICS initiative on the NDB, discussed in greater detail in Chapter 5. For now, it is simply worth noting that, although the new bank provides an alternative to the IFIs still controlled by the West, it promotes no comprehensive decoupling from the wider global economy or established institutional architecture.

The challenge of the Third World through the NIEO in the 1960s and 1970s comes closer to an accurate comparison, by recalibrating the challenge of the BRICS as connected to the discontent of the rest of the global South with an economic rather than a strategic prioritization. In terms of declaratory statements, the BRICS is commonly linked to the legacy of earlier struggles. For example, Marius Fransman, South Africa's deputy minister of international relations and cooperation, stated that:

> drawing from the important history of the origins of South–South co-operation laid down in 1955 at the Bandung Conference, as well

as with the creation of the Non-Aligned Movement in 1961, the Government of South Africa recognized that we have to be part of the forward march of history. Our accession into BRICS is also an acknowledgement of the fact that the age of globalization requires us to elevate mutual partnerships to a different level.

The deficiency in this point of comparison is that in operational practice, the BRICS marks not a transformative approach in the interest of the rest of the global South as in the 1960s and 1970s, but rather a shift to a cautious and selective problem-solving style by a specific subset of countries. Certainly, it is no exaggeration to say that through the formation and sustainability of the BRICS the process of contraction of the developing world has been finalized. Rather than representing the majority of states in the world, the BRICS members have reconfigured themselves in a highly specific forum with an exclusive, informal club culture reminiscent of forums such as the G7.

In terms of refining this image of change versus continuity, the BRICS can be linked with the special cluster of newly industrialized countries (NICs), a grouping associated with the 1960s and 1970s. By breaking the hold of the bloc ethos of Third World solidarity, in favour of an acceptance of some key tenets of globalization and the movement of trade and capital, the NICs (led by the 'Asian Tigers' of Singapore, Korea, Taiwan, and Hong Kong) opened the door to deepened economic integration so crucial to the BRICS. The NICs also created large corporations operating beyond their own national territories, with strong state leadership and a priority on developing human capital, a model that the BRICS was able to build on. The NICs, however, lacked the combination of collective mobilization or normative appeal about their role in their global system. Whether viewed as individual actors integrated in the global economy or as part of a diplomatic club through the G20 and their own stand-alone summit process, the BRICS matters today in the global system in a manner that was unavailable to the NICs.

This review of the earlier patterns of challengers to the global system is indispensable for setting the scene for scrutinizing the BRICS. Yet such an investigation highlights what the BRICS is not, more than what it is. With a distinct institutional personality, backed by a very different magnitude of economic weight, it is the unique not the generic quality of the BRICS that stands out. Such a conclusion is buttressed, in turn, by a closer examination of the distinctive means by which the BRICS operates in terms of the internal dynamic driven by its club-like approach.

Chapter 4
Hanging together

Through their communiqués and other outputs, the BRIC/BRICS countries have worked hard to present themselves as a cohesive group. This effort, however, belies sharp differences in the political, economic, and policy approaches of the member states. At a basic logistical level, unforeseen events and competing domestic priorities have at times complicated the summit process. The April 2010 Brasilia Summit, for example, was shortened to a one-day event when Chinese President Hu Jintao was required to return home to deal with a major earthquake that killed over 600 people in western China. In June 2010, a BRIC caucus meeting on the margins of the Toronto G20 was cancelled when Brazilian President Luiz Inácio Lula da Silva stayed home because of the massive floods in north-east Brazil. The 2014 BRICS summit at Fortaleza, expected to be held in March, was postponed by Brazilian president Dilma Rousseff until 15 July to coincide with the state visit of Chinese leader Xi Jinping and the finale of the FIFA World Cup.

More seriously still, as a group the BRICS countries themselves are riddled with rivalries over borders, resources, and status. There are long-standing and highly sensitive border disputes between India and China, and India is also concerned about the Chinese presence in the Indian Ocean. In addition, India still imposes some restrictions on Chinese companies investing in

India, and considers them a potential security threat. China's and India's anxiety when energy prices rise must be set against Russia's problems when they fall, while Brazil is both a cause and beneficiary of rising food prices. China's highly competitive exports inflict material harm on Brazilian and South African manufacturing sectors such as clothing and textiles. The BRICS countries are divided on the issue of reforming the UNSC, with China having some aspirations to bipolarity—through the possible creation of a so-called United States–China G2 informal institutional structure—not just a multipolar global order with greater space for the entire cast of the BRICS.

Nor do the BRICS countries always act as a concerted bloc within other informal institutional settings, even in the context of the G20, where the members commonly caucus together prior to meetings. Lines of division in the G20 are not rigid and do not adhere to traditional North–South alliances. Brazil, along with Germany and the European Union, has expressed concern over Chinese as well as American exchange rate and monetary policies. China joins with Germany in fighting off US criticism of 'global imbalances' and vigorously opposes US demands for political intervention against trade surpluses. These cross-cutting divisions starkly illustrate that cohesiveness within the BRICS has not congealed to the point where it acts as a tightly coordinated group in every situation. Open indications of this inability to act as a bloc emerged in 2011 and 2012, when the BRICS failed to mount a united campaign for the position of the managing director of the IMF or president of the World Bank.

Yet, for all of these constraints, the BRICS countries have hung together. In doing so, they have reproduced a club culture reminiscent of the dynamics of the G7, mixing self-selective membership with an emphasis on reinforcing commonalities and downplaying differences. Although both the BRICS and the G7 emerged out of periods of economic dislocation, the domestic context within the member countries at the time of each forum's creation was radically different. Created in 1975 the G7—originally the G5 with the exclusion of Italy and Canada—was created in an atmosphere of economic distress in the context of rapidly rising oil prices and economic stagflation within the core countries of the West. The BRICS, in contrast, was launched from a position of relative strength at least from the perspective of its membership amid the economic and political turmoil of the 2008 global financial crisis. Thus, while the G7 was created by a group of already powerful countries concerned about the prospect of relative economic decline, the creation of the BRICS reflected the aspirations of a group of rising states.

As a result, the communications of the BRICS' leaders at the initial summits denoted a robust sense of economic self-confidence and political assertiveness. Many of these statements focused explicitly on a process of global transition, with a strong emphasis on the emergence of a multipolar world order. In this context, cooperation among the group, alongside the economic and social dynamism of the member countries, underpinned a broader perception that the balance of power in the international system was shifting.

Internally, there is a striking degree of attention to organizational maintenance. Above all else, the BRICS exhibits a careful, safety-first mode of interaction. As Nikolas Gvosdev has put it: 'One of the advantages of the BRICS process is that it remains a loose association of states with somewhat disparate interests, so no effort is made to force a common position when the BRICS states cannot agree on one. But these states have also found a way to disagree on some key issues ... without torpedoing the entire enterprise'.

Mastering a club-like approach in terms of internal diplomacy, the BRICS members have adopted an operating model that reinforces their collective agenda in the global forums, but only when they can avoid frictions on contested issues among the individual members. Despite serious competing strategic divergences, the BRICS has been able to overcome differences by downplaying contentious issues while elevating and reinforcing the issues of members' common interest. At the same time, they have worked to avoid interinstitutional tensions by continually emphasizing the centrality of the G20 process in their joint communications. The endurance and strength of the BRICS rests on the firmly ingrained application of informal and loose club dynamics that has facilitated the group's sustainability.

BRICS momentum and constraints

The BRICS members relate to the global system with a mutually reinforcing sense of historical grievance and some claims to represent the interests of all developing countries. They share a rhetorical commitment to the defence of the Westphalian model of state sovereignty and non-intervention. They profess a shared vision of inclusive global growth, combined with development policy autonomy and the rapid socio-economic transformation of their own states. They proclaim the need for a rules-based, stable, and predictable world order that respects the diversity of political systems and stages of development. By playing up these core principles, at the expense of detailed differences on a variety of substantive issues, the BRICS members have not put their cooperation in jeopardy.

The salience of the club approach stands out when one attempts to peel away the layers of ambiguity and even contradictions, which point to the difficulties in making the BRICS more than a mix of individual parts. Unlike formal institutions such as the United Nations, the IFIs, and the WTO, the BRICS makes no attempt to negotiate, never mind impose, binding rules upon its member states. The wording of BRICS communiqués subordinates national differences to core commonalities of perspective, emphasizing converging interests and minimizing points of tension and disagreement.

The BRICS devote the highest level of attention to the cluster of issues where members can express their traditional sense of grievance at being marginalized within the global institutional architecture and their shared sense of criticism of the West's poor management of the global economy. Global financial issues receive a large amount of coverage in the summit declarations, more than expressions of solidarity with the rest of the global South, environmental and climate change issues, and promotion of the G20 and trade.

The 2008 global financial crisis gets abundant attention. The widespread adverse effect of that crisis, for which the Western establishment was responsible, had threatened to destabilize the emerging economies' vibrant growth. As a result, the crisis magnified the shared sense of injustice among the developing countries that were traditionally marginalized in the decision-making process in the IFIs. Speaking at the World Economic Forum in Davos, Chinese premier Wen Jiabao blamed the West's financial exuberance and mismanagement. In particular, Wen criticized the United States' and Europe's 'excessive expansion of financial institutions in blind pursuit of profit [and] lack of self discipline among financial institutions and ratings agencies' for causing the worst financial crisis since the Great Depression. In 2009, India's minister for petroleum and natural gas Murli Deora noted at the meeting of the SCO in Beijing that 'most of us represent developing countries, and in varying degrees, have been adversely affected by the global financial and economic crisis. The crisis began in the heart of the capitalist world but its effects have been felt across the globe.'

At the same time, BRICS members demonstrated the strength of their macroeconomic policy by dealing with the crisis effectively. The crisis thus revealed the importance of BRICS economies for progress towards global recovery and hence strengthened their legitimacy as the voice of the South. Chinese President Hu Jintao noted that:

> The steady increase of their representation and the greater say they acquired in global economic governance has moved the international order in the direction of greater fairness and rationality. What has happened testifies once again that without the rise of emerging markets and developing countries, there will be no universal prosperity in the world; and that without the stability of these countries, there will be no world peace and stability.

By way of contrast, the BRICS members remain the most divided on the issue of UNSC reform. It receives minimal media coverage in the context of BRICS summits. Downplaying such a sensitive subject is especially noteworthy because the issue of UNSC membership continually receives substantive and continuous coverage, especially in the Indian media.

Such self-restraint meshes with the notion of organizational or club maintenance, in that in other contexts India did not shy away from pressing China—a member of the Permanent Five (P5)—to support its claim to UNSC membership. China, for its part, acknowledged India's interest in the permanent membership but stopped short of supporting its bid. Brazil's stance echoed the Indian position. Rousseff noted in 2012 that 'Brazil and India strongly converge for the reform of international organisations', including 'expansion of the UN Security Council'. India and Brazil remain united in the struggle to reform the United Nations, where, together, in an enlarged Security Council, they would be able to contribute significantly to the international system, which lacks legitimacy and effectiveness in its current make-up. However, China and Russia take an equivocal position in respect to India's and Brazil's aspirations. The joint communiqué of the BRICS foreign ministers in 2008 noted, 'the Ministers of Russia and China reiterated that their countries attach importance to the status of India and Brazil in international affairs, and understand

and support India's and Brazil's aspirations to play a greater role in the United Nations'.

Magnifying similarities and playing down differences are also marked in the contrast between the amount of attention given to trade as opposed to reform of the IFIs. An analysis of converging views among the BRICS members reveals that the image of solidarity on the issue of IFI reform has grown over time. The urgent need for a fundamental transformation in IFI governance has taken centre stage at BRICS summits. At the Sanya Summit held in 2011 in China, for example, the leaders made this goal a priority, calling for 'a quick achievement of the targets for the reform of the IMF agreed to at previous G20 summits and reiterate that the governing structure of the IFIs should reflect the changes in the world economy, increasing the voice and representation of emerging economies and developing countries'.

Alternatively, downplaying trade issues masked the tensions that had opened up among the BRICS countries since the 2003 WTO ministerial in Cancún. In broad terms this split divided Brazil and South Africa, which wanted to liberalize trade in order to enhance their competitive agricultural sectors, against India, which remained more staunchly protectionist. In 2006, India's commerce minister Kamal Nath stood up to pressure for a deal on the Doha Round of trade negotiations, bluntly acknowledging that failure was better than a bad deal. At the 2013 Bali WTO ministerial, India again demonstrated willingness to go it alone so as to stop any result that did not allow raising the current ceiling on food subsidies at the national level. Both the outgoing government of Prime Minister Manmohan Singh and the incoming government of Prime Minister Narendra Modi were of a single mind that India's concerns on food security were non-negotiable, even if such a stance stymied a wider WTO agreement designed to streamline customs procedures supported by the other BRICS members.

Maintaining flexible club cohesion

A significant degree of reform has been possible without huge disruption, thanks to the privileging of new informal forums at the hub of the global institutional architecture. Whereas in the past rising powers have only been accommodated in the system after decisive wars, the BRICS has moved into pivotal positions by invitation, albeit with the galvanizing influence of the financial crisis. Indeed, the process of accommodation extended across a wide spectrum, stretching out to a number of bodies beyond the G20. The Basel Committee on Banking Supervision widened its membership to encompass China, India, Brazil, and South Africa. The Committee on the Global Financial System also added China, India, and Brazil as constituents. When the Financial Stability Forum was upgraded to the Financial Stability Board in the midst of the global financial crisis in 2009, China, India, and Brazil were included.

Within the hub of the G20, BRICS members play a hedging game, keeping their options open. They were quite willing to move into the premier forum of economic governance without preconditions or material quid pro quos. At the peak of the financial crisis they acted as responsible stakeholders, supporting most notably the massive stimulus package featured at the first three G20 summits held in Washington DC, London, and Pittsburgh. Nonetheless, while considering the G20 the prime conduit for addressing global issues, and expressing their desire that the G20's position be coordinator of the global response to the financial crisis, they did not want to lock themselves into a position that curtailed other options. While the BRICS took whatever status could be gained from membership, this approach did not translate into a form of authentic ownership or pattern of concerted activism within the G20. The BRICS remained cautiously defensive.

In orchestrating this wait-and-see approach, China stands out as the prime driving force. It kept in the background during the early stages of the formation of the group, letting Russia and Brazil move out ahead as the visible motors of the BRIC. Although China hosted the 2011 summit in Sanya, it exerted its influence behind the scenes. It did not propose any bold issue-specific initiatives, like Russia had done. In geopolitical terms, China refrained from any rhetoric that cast the BRIC as a competitor to the Western establishment. Chinese state officials presented the BRIC as a means to advance the tenets of fairness in the global system, rather than as a mechanism to open up new kinds of competition.

The BRICS club culture, which plays down areas of competition (P5 status, for example) and plays up areas of solidarity (as in IFI reform), mirrors China's own cautious approach to international institutions. The concern of the BRICS for organizational maintenance, for the most part, perfectly complements the goals of Chinese diplomacy. China took very few risks in the building of the BRIC. Unlike Russia, it did not host the first meetings. Unlike Brazil's Lula, its leaders' statements were cautious and restrained. In terms of deepening the relationship, China prefers to lead from behind, as witnessed by the creation of the NDB, when it moved into the spotlight only after India pushed ahead with the initiative.

The only exception to this model came in the widening of club membership to include South Africa. Whereas China adopted a reactive stance in terms of consolidating the BRICS, adjusting its approach to others' first moves, on expansion it was prepared to lead. While the way forward to bring South Africa into the BRICS had been prepared by other mechanisms, it is significant to note that China championed its entry into the group. Such a move completely severed the ties from the image of the BRIC as a construct of Goldman Sachs, in that South Africa was absent not only from Jim O'Neill's original concept but also from his follow-up identification of the N11 cluster of countries. It also opened up a new appreciation about identity, interest, and diplomatic leverage within BRICS.

Expanding—not downsizing the club

When the BRIC was created, the main question relating to membership involved the inclusion of Russia. For Goldman Sachs, the four big original BRIC countries had enormous appeal as the dynamic global motors of growth. On the basis of GDP and PPP, China, India, Russia, and Brazil were all in the top ten, ahead of Mexico, Indonesia, and South Africa in the top twenty-five. On other criteria as well, Russia could be cast as a good fit, with a large population, rapid urbanization, and a high level of consumerism at the upper echelons of society, episodic high growth, growing flows of FDI, expanding trade volumes, and, consequently, the fast accumulation of foreign exchange reserves.

In other ways, Russia stretched the definition of a rising state beyond credibility. Rather than emerging from the global South, it had been at the apex of power under the bipolar system during the post-1945 era. It gained superpower status as the Soviet Union in the form of a P5 seat with veto power at the United Nations. Furthermore, it was backed by a strong ideology and an array of satellite and proxy states in and beyond Eastern Europe. Despite being left out of the core economic institutions, including the IFIs and the General Agreement on Tariffs and Trade, the Soviet Union/Russia had been a serious rival to the United States and the West with a wide number of accomplishments, from the Sputnik satellites to a formidable military/industrial complex.

In the aftermath of the collapse of the USSR, Russia is more easily framed as a legacy power, or a country in decline rather than in ascendance. President Vladimir Putin calls the break-up of the Soviet Union the geopolitical catastrophe of the 20th century. With its territory shrunk by the collapse of the USSR, a declining population, and a lack of diversification in its investment and trade portfolios, Russia remains constrained in terms of its global profile and reach. Unlike the other BRICS members, Russia is a rentier state dependent on hydrocarbon production.

Notwithstanding a lack of shared economic characteristics, Russia could be included in the BRIC because of its self-image as a country worthy of—but lacking—the attributes of respect in the global system. In objective terms, Russia might look like an insider, a status bestowed by its P5 position and enhanced by its entry into the G8. But in subjective terms, Russia considered itself as much a thwarted and aspirant actor in a biased world order as China, India, or Brazil.

South Africa, by way of comparison, is substantially at odds with the size of other BRICS members in population, economy, land mass, and growth rate. Indeed, it fails to make the grade as a global rising power based on its material capabilities. Jim O'Neill remains adamant that not only does South Africa fall short of the other four countries on a quantitative basis but also that its inclusion detracts from the group's profile. These types of market-based assessments focus on Korea, Indonesia, Mexico, or Turkey rather than on South Africa. And in Africa, the N11 favours Nigeria as a country with a positive economic future.

In this context, the striking question is not why Russia remains but why South Africa was brought into the BRICS. In general terms, the argument for South Africa's entry is based on diplomatic logic. It works well with the BRIC members in a number of coalitions, such as the Heiligendamm Process and the G8 O5 process from the time of the 2005 Gleneagles Summit. This comfort level is evident as well in the formation of the BASIC group—Brazil, India, and China along with South Africa but not Russia—in relation to climate change negotiations.

In the BASIC group as in the O5, the benefits of working through a coordinating group were evident. BASIC members met regularly during the preparations for the 15th meeting of the Conference of the Parties (COP) to the UN Framework Convention on Climate Change in Copenhagen through December 2009. South Africa's bridge-building skills stood out as a major source of strength, and embellished the wish of the BRICS not to be isolated from the rest of the global South. Although South Africa, with relatively low levels of greenhouse gas emissions, takes some different positions from the other four countries, they all shared a common stance up to the time it hosted COP-17 in Durban in 2011. Indeed, it was at Durban that BASIC spoke in plenary as a 'united negotiating group'.

South Africa's geographic location is another major attraction for the original BRIC members given their concerted push for engagement with Africa. Certainly extending the South Africa relationship has a particular instrumental value for China, easing access to South Africa's own massive natural resources and allowing a conduit to the rest of Africa as part of an ambitious continental strategy. Moreover, there was reciprocal interest. South African President Jacob Zuma was granted the prospect of BRICS membership on his impressive trade tour of China in December 2010, accompanied by a delegation of seventeen cabinet members and 300 businesspeople.

Yet the material dimension should not be exaggerated. China's relationship with South Africa is complex, as it is with other African countries, carrying enormous benefits as well as risks due to a loss of manufacturing jobs from Chinese competition and possible negative spillover costs from an undervalued Chinese currency. Consistent with the diplomatic logic, the Zuma government embraced the BRICS largely because it endorses South Africa's dual credentials as a top-tier player and the representative of Africa. The first image showcases South Africa's resource endowments, highly developed infrastructure, and corporate and financial footprints into the rest of Africa. The second focuses on South Africa's credentials since 1994 with the end of the apartheid era as a lead 'voice' from the global South within the G77 and the NAM.

A long transitional moment

The loose club style allows the BRICS to project a confidence about its rise, with a considerable degree of sustainability. Biding their time and focusing on converging interests and values, BRICS members have channelled their long-standing sense of frustrated ambitions into a collective mechanism.

Such a cautious attitude is consistent with the image of the BRICS not as a radical challenger to the global system, but as a group that desires full recognition of its economic and diplomatic achievements. Well rehearsed in the context of the global financial crisis, the BRICS members contrasted their own orthodoxy to deleterious policy actions by the United States and the European Union, destabilizing actions that continued with quantitative easing by generating 'excessive liquidity' and fostered 'excessive capital flows and commodity prices'. Turning the tables, they called for the advanced economies 'to adopt responsible macroeconomic and financial policies, avoid creating excessive global liquidity and undertake structural reforms to lift growth that create jobs'.

Equally, the club approach has mitigated the prospects of the BRICS foundering as a major force in the global system not because of resistance by the old order but due to serious differences of values and interests among the group's members. Although these differences persist they have not been so obvious as to fracture the group. The ability of the BRICS to navigate change successfully was reinforced by South Africa's entry. Notwithstanding the diplomatic and material rationales for its inclusion, this move may have been detrimental to the South African–Indian–Brazilian trilateral relationship through IBSA. Any worries about this consequence, though, were kept private, as the club culture emphasized the complementary synergy between the BRICS and IBSA.

If this ability to overcome differences on widening the group's composition deserves credit, the deepening of the BRICS to allow issue-area coordination poses a more serious standard to pass. Until some form of key deliverable becomes operational, the interpretation that the BRICS is all declarations with no real tangible action is difficult to dislodge. As such the push by the BRICS to establish the NDB is extremely important.

Chapter 5
Building the New Development Bank

Brought forward by India at the 2012 BRICS Summit in New Delhi, the NDB—alternatively called the BRICS Development Bank—represents the most significant institutional innovation to emerge from the BRICS summit process. Considerable scepticism, however, has been expressed about the viability of the project. In light of the broad differences in strategic interests and economic capabilities among BRICS members—and the lack of organizational capacity available to address them—Western policymakers and a range of commentators have suggested that the ability and willingness of those five countries to deliver on the promises of the NDB may be limited.

In diplomatic terms, the perceived difficulty of creating and maintaining the NDB stemmed from the dynamics of internal competition among the BRICS countries themselves. In addition, the proposal of cooperation among the BRICS countries threatened to compete with ongoing bilateral initiatives, particularly in the case of India and China. Notwithstanding these barriers, the BRICS was able successfully to transform the proposal to establish a new international institution into concrete action. At the BRICS Fortaleza Summit in Brazil in 2014, the countries established the NDB with an initial $50 billion fund, with equal stakes provided by each of the members. At the same time, the countries agreed to establish the Contingent Reserve

Arrangement (CRA), amounting to $100 billion as a buttress against any future financial crisis.

While frustration with existing international institutions dominated by the West—and particularly the stalled process of quota reform of the IFIs—galvanized the BRICS countries' support of the NDB, much of the success in negotiating the initiative can be attributed to the flexible nature of the BRICS process, which allows for trade-offs and accommodation among the members. At the same time, the negotiating process that led to the creation of the NDB and the CRA showcased the evolving internal power dynamics of the BRICS. Although both Russia and Brazil had previously taken leadership roles in the BRICS process, the large countries and economies—specifically China and India—dominated on the specific issues raised by the NDB and the CRA.

Projecting parallel forms of global reach

The BRICS countries have made considerable strides in overcoming their own development challenges while simultaneously projecting elements of their domestic successes abroad. While these activities were traditionally conducted bilaterally, significant parallels existed among members' individual efforts. Through their development activities abroad, each displayed a mix of both soft power and hard, material objectives. While branding themselves as standing in solidarity with the global South—and thus standing apart from the countries of the West—the BRICS countries also worked to expand their access to foreign markets and natural resources.

This combination was illustrated most dramatically in BRICS members' targeting of Africa. For China, Africa represents a crucial part of its 'going out strategy', intended to direct excess savings at home towards securing assets—and particularly natural resources—abroad. In 2000, China initiated the Forum on China–Africa Cooperation (FOCAC). Diplomatically, the

scope of this exercise is best captured by reference to the third
FOCAC summit held in Beijing in October 2006, attended by
thirty-three African heads of state or government. Beijing
complemented the summit by hosting the annual general meeting
of the African Development Bank (AfDB) in Shanghai in May
2007—only the second time it met outside the African continent.
Materially, China announced $5 billion worth of concessionary
loans during the 2006 summit, an amount that was subsequently
doubled as a low-cost loan at the fourth ministerial meeting in
2009, held at Sharm el-Sheikh, Egypt, attended by forty-nine
heads of state or government.

In early 2008, India responded to the Chinese initiative, jumping
into the competition by hosting the more modest, and selective,
India–Africa Forum Summit in 2008, with fourteen African leaders.
A follow-up summit was held in Addis Ababa in 2011, an event
attended by the same number of countries. In an effort to ratchet up
its own efforts to Chinese levels, India promised a $5 billion credit
line in 2008 and a three-year credit line of $5 billion to promote its
development goals in 2011.

Ad hoc outreach efforts by individual BRICS countries reinforced
bilateral relations with Africa. Chinese President Hu Jintao
toured Africa three times after 2003. The most ambitious of
these trips occurred in February 2007 and encompassed eight
countries. With the change of leadership in November 2012,
this pattern was extended in a similarly ambitious manner.
Xi Jinping, within a week of the National People's Congress that
formalized his appointment as president, took his inaugural
trip aboard, combining visits to Russia and a number of African
countries (Tanzania, South Africa, and the Republic of
Congo), on his way to the BRICS summit in Durban. Chinese
premier Li Keqiang followed up with another extensive trip to
Africa—covering Nigeria, Angola, Ethiopia, and Kenya—in
May 2014. Among a long list of announcements, Li delivered
a $10 billion credit line to African countries for mutually

agreed projects, as well as \$2 billion for the China–Africa Development Fund.

Other BRICS leaders made similar forays. Prime Minister Manmohan Singh of India attended the 2011 India–Africa Summit in Addis Ababa as part of a concerted attempt to catch up with China. President Vladimir Putin of Russia visited South Africa in September 2006—the first trip by a Russian leader to sub-Saharan Africa since the fall of the Soviet Union. Although with heavy symbolic overlays, the signing of the Treaty on Friendship and Partnership was accompanied by a range of intergovernmental agreements as well as large-scale agreements between large corporations of both countries. Brazilian President Luiz Inácio Lula da Silva's targeting of Africa went even further, encompassing nine visits to Africa with the first one taking place in November 2003, when he conducted a five-country tour in the company of some one hundred members of the Brazilian business community. In 2010, Lula concluded his eight years as president with a final extended tour of six African countries.

Whereas these types of high-profile diplomatic forays formed the basis of the relationship between Africa, the BRICS, and the rest of the global South, the national development banks of the individual BRICS members provided ongoing points of connection. The expanding reach of the BRICS countries as donors has received increasing scrutiny in recent years, with a fuller appreciation of how these states have mobilized their accumulated large foreign currency reserves at a global level. Using a broad definition of development aid that includes grants, no-interest loans, and concessional loans tied to economic cooperation from the two large Chinese state policy banks—the Export-Import Bank of China (Eximbank) and the China Development Bank (CDB)—China has already moved up to the position of the world's second-largest bilateral donor, calculated to be in the range of \$20–3 billion for 2010. India's Technical and Economic Cooperation Programme, run through the Economic

Division of the Ministry of External Affairs, has an operating budget of just over $10 billion. Moreover, India—through its export-import bank—offers lines of credit to a variety of different actors, including development banks and states, with a particular emphasis on Africa.

Brazil, although it eschews the language of official development because it is associated with an asymmetrical relationship between the North and South, has made similar dramatic strides in development cooperation. It doubled its official development assistance between 2007 and 2008 and tripled it between 2009 and 2010, raising the level to about $50 billion a year. By 2012 the Brazilian Development Bank (BNDES) had become involved with projects valued between $7 and $8 billion in Mozambique, Angola, Guinea, South Africa, and Ghana.

Moving towards collective initiatives

The dynamics that drive the shift from activities initiated by individual BRICS countries to collective initiatives are important to sketch out. In terms of instrumental rationale, the functional motivation to set up the NDB was to fill the gap in the existing architecture of global governance created by insufficient resources for infrastructure development throughout the global South. From this critical perspective, the established institutions, above all the World Bank but also the AfDB and other regional funding bodies, have not met these pressing needs. There was a demand, therefore, for an effective alternative institution to mobilize finance for infrastructure in the developing world.

But the initiative was also stimulated by the relationship between the BRICS and the IBSA Dialogue Forum, the other informal grouping of India, Brazil, and South Africa formed in the early 2000s. Although a much lower profile body than the BRICS, with a smaller membership that excludes China and Russia, IBSA had moved ahead in some areas of leadership. In terms of a substantive agenda, its most significant programme constituted the creation in March 2004 of the IBSA Facility for the Alleviation of Poverty and Hunger, which is a fund to which each member contributed $1 million. Supported by the United Nations Office for South–South Cooperation, the IBSA fund helps identify projects and best practices for poverty reduction. It is minimal in comparison to the bilateral development programmes of the BRICS and IBSA members on an individual basis, but it was nonetheless welcomed by a number of countries of the global South and received the UN's 'South–South and Triangular Cooperation Champions Award'. A wide number of countries including Burundi, Cape Verde, Guinea-Bissau, Haiti, and Cambodia have benefited from it.

Although never a competitor to a development bank on its own, the IBSA Fund demonstrates the type of initiative demanded by countries in the global South. Indeed, it is significant that it was not China but rather India—a member of IBSA as well as the BRICS—that took the lead in finding innovative development financing. Singh could build on his own extensive background as chief economic adviser, reserve bank governor, and head of the Planning Commission, as well as his role as secretary-general of the South Commission, to champion such efforts. The initiative held considerable importance for him, in that it complemented his calls for reform with the established IFIs. However, it was also attractive from a self-help perspective, because India continued to be constrained by the lack of developmental financing of its own, as illustrated most dramatically in 2012 when more than 600 million Indians were affected in the world's largest power outage.

India's entry into the G20 at the leaders' level created greater opportunity for institutional innovation. At the Seoul Summit in November 2010, Singh argued for the use of a different sort of tool to foster infrastructure development. Faced with the challenge of massive imbalances, he proposed a new institutional instrument for recycling surplus savings into investment. If at the outset

Singh was content to work through the established multilateral development banks, frustration quickly mounted because of the stalled process of IFI reform. After being reassured by the G20's commitment to transform the IFIs to accommodate the rising states from the global South, the recalcitrance of individual countries in the West to act moved the BRICS position from raising concerns about the legitimacy deficit to seeking alternatives. Although all the BRICS members were dissatisfied with the lack of progress, India's sensitivity was heightened by the fact that it had been stymied on its pursuit of a permanent seat on the UN Security Council.

Given this context, it was not surprising that India made the establishment of a new development bank the pivotal agenda item at the BRICS summit it hosted in March 2012 in New Delhi. The finance ministers' meeting held just prior to the summit made this initiative a priority. And, signalling the extension of the BRICS from an exclusive state-centric club to a wider network, the 2012 BRICS Academic Forum—which included the leading Indian think tank Observer Research Foundation (ORF)—recommended that the summit should study 'the establishment and operational modalities of financial institutions such as a Development Bank and/or an Investment Fund that can assist in the development of BRICS and other developing countries'.

However, the risks inherent in establishing such a bank tempered enthusiasm from the outset. Although India provided intellectual leadership, China possessed the structural capacity to determine if, when, and how the proposal would ultimately be implemented. This imbalance in capacity, to be sure, went beyond India and China dynamics. Indeed, it was especially pronounced in the case of the South Africa–China relationship. Although the ORF downplayed the tension, the creation of the NDB threatened to divide BRICS members into 'haves' and 'have-nots' according to economic weight and financial resources available for the project.

China did not directly block the establishment of the NDB, but its ambivalent reaction to India's initial proposal slowed the process of negotiation and institutional creation. Above all else, it wanted to ensure that any BRICS-created institution would not be at odds with its own national interests. Through a protracted technical stage, China worked to grab some of the ideational momentum away from India. After the New Delhi Summit, and in the context of the work of the ORF, the discussion shifted away from big ideas towards more technical details, which allowed China to jump into the process in an increasingly assertive and detailed manner. Prior to a gathering of BRICS finance ministers during the annual meeting of the IMF and World Bank in Tokyo in October 2012, China brought together officials, economists, and members of think tanks from the five BRICS countries to refine proposals for the development bank at a meeting in Chongqing. More generally, it quickly became clear that the development bank initiative would remain stalled until China felt sufficiently satisfied about the details to give it the green light. Xu Qinghong, section chief of the Banking Supervision Department at the China Banking Regulatory Commission, noted:

> There are vast differences between us…Looking at the history of other multilateral institutions, I think such a feasibility study will take a long time and it may test our patience. Since the Delhi Summit, so far in China there have been a lot of doubts about a proposal.

While mindful of the details, China nevertheless clearly had an incentive to support the creation of an effective banking institution. Alongside the CRA, the NDB eased the way to using China's renminbi rather than the US dollar. More symbolically, the creation of a new institution helped bolster the image of a new bargain between China, the BRICS, and the rest of the global South. The multilateralism of development could offset the growing backlash against Chinese investment abroad. Given the extraordinary scale of activity from China's Eximbank and CDB, charges of a new form of neocolonialism inevitably emerged in the context of China's involvement in Africa.

Notwithstanding China's concerted effort to present itself as a model partner for the rest of the global South, it was increasingly encountering a negative response from many directions. At the local level, Hu Jintao's scheduled trip to Zambia's copper belt during his 2007 tour was cancelled because of possible protests. At the technical and bureaucratic levels, Lamido Sanusi, governor of the Central Bank of Nigeria, in an interview in the *Financial Times*, said that China was 'a major contributor to the de-industrialisation of Africa and thus African underdevelopment'.

For its part, South Africa also supported the initiative. The proposal and the country's inclusion complemented South Africa's broader ambition to enhance its development profile in the rest of Africa. It was not in the same league as China or the other BRICS countries in terms of projection and resources, but it demonstrated its capacity by earmarking—largely through the South African Development Partnership Agency—just under $1 billion in development assistance. The concept was also popular within the Brazilian Development Bank, which viewed it as complementing its strategy for promoting economic development.

Outside the BRICS, the reaction to the proposal for a new development bank was enthusiastic. Economists Mattia Romani, Nicholas Stern, and Joseph Stiglitz endorsed the idea in a letter to the *Financial Times* on 5 April 2012, arguing that if such a bank possessed the 'full range of necessary instruments', it could boost investment significantly 'by reducing and sharing risk and generating mutual confidence between host country and investor'.

The club model and delivery of the NDB

Despite the declaratory statement at the New Delhi Summit that outlined a 'BRICS-led' South–South development bank, debate about the operational structure of the bank dragged on. The question of resource contributions from the BRICS states represented an early and significant stumbling block. From the 2012 summit on, Indian officials backed a plan to raise an initial $50 billion via equal contributions of $10 billion from each BRICS member. Brazil supported the Indian proposal for equal contributions. Conversely, China proposed that BRICS members contribute according to their overall economic capacity. Russia initially backed the Indian proposal, but by the time of the Durban Summit in 2013 it supported China's.

Difficulties in finding common ground on a funding model reflected the underlying structural asymmetry in the economic capacity of the BRICS members (see Figure 7). A contribution of $10 billion was a small measure for China, which has a GDP that outstrips the four other BRICS members combined. But it would be a serious test for South Africa to raise that amount: $10 billion is 2.5 per cent of its GDP. South Africa only agreed because this initiative was considered a priority for financing both its own infrastructure projects and those promoted in Africa more generally.

Moreover, at that meeting in Chongqing in 2012, Xu Qinghong expressed his concern that 'non-economic factors' might hinder the creation of the NDB. For sure, non-economic factors lurked behind the intensive bargaining between China and India. China's stance often put India on the defensive. There was speculation, for instance, that China was willing to pay part of the shares of other BRICS members and might thus take a leading role in safeguarding and advancing its own political interests. From an Indian perspective, this response exacerbated the unequal relationship with China. India worried that China's dominance might eventually make the bank's decision-making more like the IFIs and overshadow the voting rights and interests of the other members. India even explored the idea of offering the advanced economies a minority stake (between 40 per cent and 45 per cent) to offset China's overarching role.

7. The BRICS set up a Development Bank. The five BRICS members may not all have the same capacity to contribute $10 billion for the New Development Bank.

A second contentious issue related to the location of the headquarters of the bank. While this was not a major source of debate at the outset, as the initiative slowly took shape the tension grew as the decision on location became equated with the exercise of overall control. China, India, and South Africa all wanted to host the NDB. India played up its role as the inspirational force behind the bank, with Singh expressing pride at Durban that 'one of the ideas that we first discussed at New Delhi, that of instituting a mechanism to recycle surplus savings into infrastructure investments in developing countries, has been given a concrete shape'. Yet the other BRICS members did not share India's assumption that ideational inspiration should—and could—translate into physical ownership. In light of its economic weight, China took the view that the headquarters should be in Shanghai, a position that was championed by key Chinese think tanks. The Financial Research Centre at Fudan University argued soon after the New Delhi Summit that 'China should strive to become the headquarters of the BRICS bank'. At the other end of the spectrum, South Africa lobbied hard for the headquarters backed up by the 'in Africa' symbolism fortified by the strength of South African financial institutions.

Such contestation over control spilled over to the question of the currency to be used in the NDB's operation. The memorandum of agreement signed at New Delhi opened the way for the BRICS national development banks to extend loans denominated in their respective currencies. The process of moving away from the US dollar led to speculation about Chinese control through the internationalized renminbi, especially as China had an incentive to advocate the use of its own currency to offset currency risks in development finance. Indian finance officials were reported to have expressed the view that the bank's goal had become a means of 'legitimizing' the use of Chinese currency overseas.

The final major issue to be negotiated rested on the mode of governance for the NDB. BRICS members have been divided over whether the NDB would lend to BRICS members only or to non-members as well. China and South Africa pushed to open up the client base beyond BRICS members; India and Brazil—looking to meet needs at home—wanted a more concentrated focus within the group. Indeed, while India and Brazil prioritized building their own infrastructural capacity, China primarily sought alternative and less sensitive means to finance development projects on a global basis.

Despite their differences, the BRICS members made great progress in finalizing the initial groundwork for the NDB. The club culture of their summits allowed members to work without any pressure of rigid institutional hurdles such as the organizational problems, deadlines, influence from fragmented or bureaucratic interest groups, and turf fighting witnessed within formal institutions. The aim of the BRICS members for greater recognition of their emerging power and status from Western countries, together with the desire to strengthen cooperation despite mutual differences, were powerful political motivations.

Thus in the interval between the 2013 Durban and the 2014 Fortaleza summits, the design of the NDB was refined. A number of crucial caucus meetings took place on the sidelines of other forums, most notably the mini-summit held immediately prior to the G20's St Petersburg Summit in September 2013. By the Fortaleza Summit in July 2014, the proposal for the bank had been transformed into what appeared to be an agreeable, workable format for the BRICS countries.

The club culture of BRICS enabled the members to remain cohesive even under stress. Yet maintaining organizational cohesion was predicated on China consolidating its position as the dominant actor by ensuring that the NDB reflected its own national priorities. The BRICS adhered to the original model, with initial capital of $50 billion from equal contributions from each member, but it decided that in a few years time, in tune with China's more ambitious approach, the new bank would move towards achieving a maximum, so-called authorized, capital of $100 billion.

In an even more evident sign of supremacy, China secured the location of the bank in Shanghai. A good case could be made that Shanghai deserved this honour, given that, as Russian finance minister Anton Siluanov noted, the city has impressive infrastructure, offers opportunities to capture private funding, and is home to more investors than the other options. But it was China's own heft—not logic—that achieved the decision. Certainly this victory did not come without a struggle, as Indian officials fought long and hard for New Delhi to be the headquarters. Yet ultimately China did not concede, although it was willing to be flexible on other aspects of the BRICS bank.

China's willingness to concede on other issues facilitated a process of trading concessions within BRICS. India remained sensitive about losing out on the location of the headquarters, and about the wider implications of the power dynamics for the future workings of the NDB, but was compensated in other ways. It received the first term of the presidency for five years, followed by five-year terms for Brazil (which received the first chair of the board of directors) and Russia (which received the first chair of the board of governors). Significantly, these concessions were enabled by Brazil, as host country, not pushing its own interests. Brazil acted as a facilitator, not a competitor—a role that it played successfully. As one Brazilian diplomat stated: 'We pulled it off 10 minutes before the end of the game. We reached a balanced package that is satisfactory to all.'

Still, some issues remain among the BRICS countries. India—the World Bank's largest cumulative borrower—is concerned that the NDB will result in a radical shift away from the IFIs. At a meeting with World Bank president Jim Yong Kim in Delhi a week after the Fortaleza Summit, Prime Minister Narendra Modi noted that the World Bank's knowledge and expertise remained vital for his country. Brazil adopted a similar approach to the IMF, with Dilma Rousseff reiterating at the summit that 'we have no interest in giving up the IMF—on the contrary, we are interested in democratizing it, making it more representative'.

For China, in contrast, the NDB is a way to avoid the IFIs. With an impressive combination of material resources and diplomatic leverage, it can move beyond the bank through other initiatives. A striking case in point is its parallel initiative to establish the Asian Infrastructure Investment Bank (AIIB). Established on 24 October 2014, with twenty-one Asian countries as founding members, the AIIB promises to address Asia's abundant needs for infrastructure development. Given its size and China's lead role, this initiative could easily eclipse the institutional heft of the NDB in the long run, which would further undermine the political incentives for India, Brazil, Russia, and South Africa to cooperate in establishing the NDB. However, China's establishment of the AIIB has not hindered the promotion of the NDB. And with the ambit of the NDB extending to the rest of the global South beyond Asia, China and the other BRICS members have considerable incentive to stay engaged. As Russian central bank governor Elvira Nabiullina commented in the lead-up to the 2015 Ufa Summit, 'I don't think there's less energy [around the BRICS bank], we didn't feel that. To the contrary…all the…countries [remain] very motivated to reach speedy practical results.'

Significantly, India has played down the AIIB. It sent its joint secretary in the ministry of finance to the foundational meeting in October 2014, attended by the finance ministers from several other countries and chaired by China. Nor has India allocated any contribution in its budget, whereas it has initiated its commitment for the NDB. In large part, its stance is conditioned by its reluctance to choose sides, in that the United States objects to the establishment of the AIIB (although a number of its closest allies are willing to become members). But this differentiated approach is also conditioned by principle, because in the NDB—unlike the AIIB—the BRICS countries are equal partners.

Applying mortar to the BRICS?

The most common criticism of the BRICS is that it lacks mortar to keep its constituent parts together. Its members may find common cause in voicing their resentment about the inequalities in the global system, but their differences in identity, interests, and material conditions will likely prevent them from moving beyond this to take collective action.

The move to establish the NDB belies this assessment. The immediate impact of the new initiative should not be overstated—in resource terms it remains far behind the IFIs, both in terms of the NDB's $50 billion in subscribed capital and the CRA's

$100 billion pool versus the World Bank's $233 billion in subscribed capital and the IMF's $755 billion in liquidity (in January 2015 it had 233,688 million in special drawing rights, or $322,489 million). Yet it nonetheless represents a major achievement and a step forward for the BRICS as a substantive player in the global arena.

From the perspective of economic capacity, the BRICS members demonstrated that they could lever their material capabilities into common policy outputs. Each country had different motivations for making this type of commitment. For China, the NDB provides an opportunity to alter perceptions of its self-interested external development strategy by signalling that it could work with the other BRICS members. Russia put aside its initial reluctance about the NDB proposal, driven largely by geopolitical reasons, as solidarity through the BRICS helped balance its worsening relations with the West because of the Crimea and Ukraine. For South Africa, India, and Brazil, the proposal raises the prospect of being both borrowers and lenders to the new bank. The strain on South Africa may have been the greatest in coming up with its capital allocation, but the country's possible gains were also the most significant, as highlighted by the fact that it was the only country to gain a regional office of the bank.

From the perspective of building the BRICS group and maintaining its internal club culture, the NDB was a significant success. To China, winning the prize of the bank headquarters was worth the risk of compromising its leading-from-behind strategy. Once that goal was achieved, China quickly reverted to a more quiet, team-centred approach and displayed a willingness to distribute other types of institutional rewards on an even basis. President Xi Jinping expressed this dynamic of overall commonalities trumping specific tensions well: 'The BRICS countries may have different views on certain issues', he said. 'But such diversity and differences should and can motivate rather than impede complementary and inclusive BRICS cooperation.'

Framed as an explicit challenge to the established international institutions—and particularly the IFIs—the character and significance of the BRICS bank is more ambiguous. With respect to its concrete impact on global governance, one cluster of analyses views the NDB as an early harbinger of a new world order where emerging powers advance their own agenda through institutional innovation while shunning the existing Bretton Woods institutions of the World Bank and IMF. In contrast, other analysts question the capacity and willingness of the BRICS countries to implement and operate the NDB effectively. In this vein, Takehiko Nakao, president of the Asian Development Bank, points out that 'setting up banking business is not easy as it involves finding new projects, financing them and then monitoring the use of these funds and repayments'.

Moreover, although the countries have made serious progress since the proposal for the NDB was first introduced in 2012, significant questions remain. Civil society representatives both within and outside the BRICS states are concerned about the bank's transparency, openness, and accountability. It may represent a novel institutional innovation, but it appears unlikely to transform South–South relations or break completely with past practices. The bank remains a state-centred—and thus relatively traditional—international institution despite its system of equal funding and rotation of key administrative positions. Indeed, in its current form the NDB does not transcend beyond the state-to-state level, and makes no mention of engagement with, or accountability to, civil society. As such, the credibility of both the NDB and the broader BRICS process is increasingly questioned by civil society groups. One Brazilian activist described the conundrum between the breakthrough from the top down, and the neglect from the bottom up: 'The fact that [the BRICS countries] are pressing for a new balance of power in the world has to be stressed as a positive thing ... But where are the poor?'

Chapter 6
BRICS as the recognition of states, not societies

The BRICS, at its core, is a state-centric project. To a considerable extent, it constitutes a stylized performance in which the BRICS countries represent themselves as rising states. The emphasis is on the assertion—and granting—of a heightened degree of recognition within the global system. The motivations combine the symbolic elements, such as the aspirations for an enhanced status, and the instrumental, with respect to gaining additional policy leverage in global affairs. The summits themselves remain firmly state-orchestrated, across the spectrum from the spectacle generated by the gatherings at the leader level to the technocratic orientation of the meetings between a continually expanding cohort of state officials.

This state-centric bias reflects many of the special characteristics of the BRICS. In terms of foundational norms, BRICS members are all strong proponents of the defence of sovereignty and the principle of non-intervention. All, to a greater or lesser extent, have a strong element of state control over the economy. State-owned enterprises are at the core of the Chinese and Russian systems, often located in monopolistic or oligopolistic sectors. Notwithstanding the high profile of private companies in Brazil (Vale, Embraer), India (Tata, Reliance), and South Africa (De Beers), these countries are also home to a number of state-owned enterprises. Brazil has Petrobras, Eletrobras, and

Caixa Econômica Federa; India has Air India, Bharat Petroleum, Bank of India, and the Steel Authority of India as so-called public sector undertakings; and South Africa has Broadband Infraco, Eskom, SAFCOL, and Telkom SA, to name a few.

Conversely, the governments of individual BRICS countries have demonstrated suspicion about the activities of civil society organizations, and especially the role of transnational non-governmental organizations (NGOs). This sense of distrust with respect to civil society is unsurprising in Russia and China, where concern has been enhanced by the colour revolutions in the former states of the Soviet Union and the 'Arab Spring'. But the view at the state level that transnational civil society is not to be trusted on issues of national interest is ingrained in the other BRICS members as well. India has faced off with a number of NGOs, including Greenpeace International. Soon after Narendra Modi was elected prime minister, the government decreed that the central bank must approve any international financial transfers to the NGO. In Brazil, although relations between the state and civil society improved generally when Luiz Inácio Lula da Silva was president, major disagreements remain over deforestation of the Amazon and other areas of environmental protection. And South Africa has gone through a period of bitter contention over President Jacob Zuma's introduction of the Protection of State Information Act, which NGOs and other critics consider an attack on transparency and freedom of expression.

Still, while the state centrism of the BRICS summits to some extent mirrors the orientation of its member governments, it is also congruent with a broader generalized pattern across informal institutions, such as the G7 and G20. Because small, self-selective groups emphasize a club culture, a sense of restricted participation develops within the hierarchy of states as well as from strict barriers between insiders and outsiders where state and society intersect. The hold of exclusivity has been the hallmark of these privileged forums, which start as meetings for finance ministers and are then elevated to the summit level of leaders, as in the case of the G7 and G20, or start as foreign ministers' and leaders' meetings in the case of the BRICS. Dominated by a top–down mode of operation with respect to summitry, with leaders surrounded by only a small number of advisers (most notably the sherpas), the BRICS no less than the G7 and G20 act autonomously from societal activity.

Whatever the attractions of this elite-oriented approach, however, there is a strong argument for opening up the BRICS to broader participation on the part of societal actors. Other exclusive and informal clubs, notably the G7, have witnessed a gradual opening up to a more diverse set of participants over time, including a greater focus on civil society dialogue and the inclusion of high-profile celebrity activists. While this gradual opening up to some extent reflects growing societal opposition to the summits themselves—as witnessed by large-scale protests at the G7/8 and G20 summits—it also represents an acknowledgement by policymakers that some degree of participation by a wider set of actors is needed if the summits are to move from 'talking shops' to operational hubs.

While exclusive and limited meetings hold certain advantages—status, like-mindedness, and opportunities to further consolidate club culture—a more loose and inclusive approach is often required to gain and maintain the institution's legitimacy. On this basis, there is already some evidence that the BRICS summits are moving towards a more diffuse and porous mode of operation with the inclusion of certain societal groups, thereby building a broader 'network constituency' supportive of the summit process.

This shift is visible in efforts aimed at increasing engagement with business and trade groups and through the expansion of think tank activity connected with the summits. At the same time, the BRICS remains a firmly state-centred project and counter-trends—most notably the increasing focus on national security issues—are also evident. As cooperation among the countries continues to evolve, the tension between exclusivity and inclusion is likely to form a central debate within and among the BRICS countries themselves.

Owning the project at the state level

Understanding the context of informal institutions is a useful starting point for exploring how the BRICS has evolved in terms of comparative state–societal dynamics. The emergence of the G20 is commonly portrayed as a breakthrough in terms of equality between the traditional Western establishment and a cluster of non-Western ascendant states. The G20 summit process departed from the subordinated treatment accorded to the outreach countries by the G7 and from the outset operated on a foundation of formal equality, with no special or differentiated forms of membership. Indeed, such a breakthrough contributed to the positive perception of the G20 not only compared to the more restrictive G7, but also to the whole array of formal institutions with built-in inequality such as through the Permanent Five members of the UNSC and the asymmetrical distribution of voice and votes at the IMF. David Held, a leading theorist of cosmopolitanism, could therefore be optimistic that the G20 forum featured 'an unprecedented successful attempt by developing countries to extend their participation in key institutions of global governance'.

However convincing, this optimistic appraisal is somewhat diminished by a closer examination of the details about the G20's formation and operation. The creation of the G20 was not spearheaded by the BRICS or other countries outside of the G7. The actors in command were the same self-selected countries that had been leading over many decades—first and foremost the United States, aided by its inner circle of other G7 countries. Control of the G20 process was kept within a tight Anglo-American condominium through the first three summit meetings, with the United States hosting the first summit in Washington DC in

November 2008, the United Kingdom hosting the second in London in April 2009, and the United States returning to the host function in Pittsburgh in September 2009.

Furthermore, in terms of the substantive agenda the G20 did not demonstrate any explicit change of control by the United States and the West. The initial stages privileged the old establishment in hosting, in selecting members, and in setting the agenda. While it is true that this image of embedded empowerment began diminishing by the November 2010 Seoul Summit, the sensitivities that opened up at the creation of the G20 between the old establishment and the BRICS continued to inform behaviour, with the United States/West continuing to act as though they owned the G20 and the BRICS playing a more reactive and defensive role.

The diluted representation of the BRICS within the G20 exacerbated this sensitivity about control. When the suggestion of an explicit concert between the old establishment and the ascendant big states of the global South was mooted, the United States favoured a more inclusive approach. The BRICS countries were brought into the inner circle hub of the G20, but they were not alone—the United States in particular adopted a 'the bigger the better' strategy. This widening could be justified by the existence of the G20 finance forum, so the membership could be brought in off the shelf. As such, the BRICS members suspected that the choice of any other members brought into the G20 was largely driven by geopolitical interests, with little consideration of whether they shared the same systemic importance as the BRICS members.

Building on the model of informal institutions, extended from the G7 to the G20, appealed to the BRICS members. At the same time, the creation of a forum of their own—with similar design elements but autonomous from the existing 'G' groupings—became increasingly compelling. This approach offered an organized site to which the individual big rising states could belong, without having to adapt to an organizational format not of their making. Moreover, the BRICS could embrace this autonomous option without having to exit the G20. The BRICS members could both signal their independence as outsiders and, at the same time, act as insiders.

In terms of global profile, the BRICS countries reaped huge dividends through these innovative, dualistic modes of informal institutionalism. They could be released from the legacy of subordination vis-à-vis the G7 without taking on the role of 'irresponsible stakeholders'. The move to take on an actual diplomatic personality allowed the BRICS to take the spotlight with its own summit meeting. While without fail participating in the G20 (even amid the controversy about Russian president Vladimir Putin's attendance at the Brisbane Summit in 2014), the BRICS could tune the culture of informality to their own interests and identities. Indeed, while being careful not to take on the role of overt spoilers in the G20, the BRICS made some considerable effort to differentiate its own summit process in terms of the allocation of leadership responsibilities.

Leadership from the front was played down in terms of hosting. Whereas the United States hosted the first and the third of the G20 summits, China only hosted the third in the cycle of the BRICS summits. And unlike the G7/8, with a set rotation of summits, the BRICS allows improvisation. In terms of hosting, Brazil went ahead of Russia to host the 2014 summit (with Russia preferring to move back a year as it had taken on the hosting functions of APEC (Asia-Pacific Economic Cooperation) in 2012, the G20 in 2013, and, until it was cancelled because of the Crimea crisis, the G8 in 2014). In terms of timing, Brazil shifted the date of the Fortaleza Summit forward from March to the middle of July to accommodate the staging of the FIFA World Cup.

Moreover, no single national leader stands out as the dominant animator, a fact underscored by the fact that both the first unofficial and official BRICS summits were hosted by 'caretaker' Russian President Dmitry Medvedev (not Vladimir Putin, who had moved to the position of prime minister after his constitutionally limited term as president ended in 2008).

These signs of differentiation notwithstanding, the BRICS remains largely a replica of the generic set of design elements seen across other informal summits. As with the original 'G' summits the state centrism of BRICS is reinforced by its mode of operation. The communiqués of BRICS are kept short, and what is left out is as significant as what is included. The priority continues to be organizational maintenance through the discipline of the built-in club culture. Although sharing a declaratory commitment to democratize the global system and major international organizations, the BRICS is both constrained and guarded about the extent of its own organizational transparency.

In terms of composition, the leaders limit the size of their entourages for the summit process. Reproducing the model of the G7/8 and G20, and keeping the analogy of mountain climbing, the key advisers to the leaders are the sherpas, who do the bulk of the preparatory work and act as guides and porters. The individuals appointed to this position are savvy and trusted technocrats. In the Russian case, Yevgeny Primakov—a prominent realist academic, and Russia's former foreign minister (1996–8) and prime minister (1998–9)—stood out. Primakov has been identified by Russian commentators as the authentic founding father of the BRIC/BRICS, both because of his proposal during his visit to New Delhi in 1998 of a strategic triangle between RIC, and because of his assertion during an extensive trip in 1997 to Latin America that Brazil could become a major Russian ally in the construction of a multipolar world.

Certainly, Primakov continued to inform Russian strategic thinking on the BRIC/BRICS in the background as he became the president of the Russian Chamber of Commerce and Industry and a member of the Russian Academy of Sciences. But the role of sherpa at the initial Yekaterinburg Summit was given to Arkady Dvorkovich, an economic adviser to Medvedev, who took on the analogous role at the G20 Washington Summit before becoming deputy prime minister in 2012. Similarly, the profile of the Russian sherpa did not rise appreciably under Putin, after he returned to office in 2012, as he appointed Sergei Rybakov, a deputy foreign minister, as his sherpa for the 2014 Fortaleza Summit.

This low-key technocratic orientation was accented by the type of appointment for the Indian, Brazilian, Chinese, and South African sherpas. Prime Minister Manmohan Singh's sherpa for the 2012 New Delhi Summit was Sudhir Vyas, secretary of economic relations in India's Ministry of External Affairs, an able bureaucrat but one without the policy clout of Montek Singh Ahluwalia, Singh's choice as his G20 sherpa. A similar approach can be detected in the case of the other members. At the 2011 Sanya Summit the Chinese sherpa was assistant foreign minister Wu Hailong, another highly competent bureaucrat but a state official lacking the high profile of He Yafe, who was President Hu Jintao's sherpa at the G20 Washington Summit. At both the 2009 Yekaterinburg and 2010 Brasilia summits, Roberto Jaguaribe, undersecretary-general for political affairs at Brazil's Ministry of External Relations, served as Lula's sherpa. Although clearly possessing the president's trust, once again the contrast is striking between the choice of Jaguaribe as BRICS sherpa and that of Antonio Aguiar Patriota (who took on this role from Washington where he was Brazil's ambassador to the United States) as the sherpa for the Washington G20.

The only BRICS member that has deviated from this pattern was South Africa. Ambassador Jerry Matjila—a senior career diplomat both with the African National Congress in exile and in the new post-1994 South Africa was President Jacob Zuma's sherpa from the 2011 Sanya through to the 2015 Ufa summit. Although attracting subsequent controversy for his role as director-general of the department of international relations and co-operation, he was a low-key BRICS sherpa. By contrast, Alan Hirsch, the chief economist in the presidency's policy unit, served as a high profile G20 sherpa, highlighted by his appointment as the co-chair of the G20 Development Working Group from 2010 to 2012.

Opening up the BRICS? Pressure and resistance

The logic of bending, if not breaking, the state centrism of BRIC/BRICS has become more pronounced over time. Some moves towards a broader recognition of interests and societal actors were apparent early on in the formative process of the BRICS summits. For example, in their 2008 communiqué, the BRIC foreign ministers stressed the salience of tackling societal problems in the form of 'acute global problems of our time, such as poverty, hunger and diseases'. Nevertheless, advances in response to the claims of societal forces to participate in the process have not emerged easily. Instead of embracing civil society groups as integral partners, the operational approach was predicated on the principle that 'due account [be] taken of the interests of all nations'.

The first three BRIC summits attracted little in the way of a societal response, with their relatively low diplomatic profile and physical location away from major metropolitan areas—in Yekaterinburg, Brasilia, and Sanya. Civil society was more sceptical of the importance of the BRICS than actively resistant to the concept. As a result, over this period a significant divide emerged between deepening engagement between BRICS state officials and the relative detachment evident among domestic non-governmental groupings. In contrast to the growing backlash against the excess associated with BRIC/BRICS enthusiasm at the state level for hosting major sporting events—whether the Olympics in China and Russia, the Commonwealth Games in India, or the FIFA World Cup in South Africa and Brazil—BRICS summits operated below the public radar.

Growing protests within the BRICS states both foreshadowed the emergence of a more concerted opposition to the BRICS summits and highlighted a growing gap between the increasing influence of the member countries on the global stage and their relative success in meeting the rising expectations of their own populations with respect to domestic governance. Indeed, while the creation of the BRIC(S) stemmed from a desire on the part of the member countries for an improved system of global governance that provided enhanced recognition and voice on the basis of their new power and status, weaknesses in attributes of national governance persisted. In this context, ethical gaps and corruption served to exacerbate the impact of the massive socio-economic inequalities present within the BRICS countries.

It is illuminating from this perspective that, in the midst of the formative years of BRICS, each member has been hit by major scandals. Brazil has witnessed two serious political corruption cases, one known as the 'mensalao' vote-buying scandal during Lula's government and another an escalating kickback scheme at Brazil's state-run oil company Petrobras, which has seriously undermined support for the government of Dilma Rousseff. Scandals in India have included corrupt deals of overstated contracts for the 2010 Commonwealth Games and the illegal undercharging by government officials to various telecom companies during the allocation of mobile phone licences.

In Russia, massive corruption allegations came to the fore over construction projects for the APEC summit and the Winter Olympic Games in Sochi, as well as an embezzlement scandal over the Russian Space Systems project related to a satellite navigation system dubbed GLONASS. Chinese authorities seized assets worth approximately $14.5 billion from the family members and associates of retired domestic security tsar Zhou Yongkang, although the sentence of life in prison imposed on Zhou for taking bribes and other offences is as much an indication of a political power struggle as the seriousness of the crackdown against both 'tigers and flies'—meaning officials at all levels—in an anti-corruption campaign. And South Africa's Jacob Zuma has been accused of using $24 million in public monies on lavish upgrades to his private home in Nkandla, KwaZulu-Natal.

The first sign of an active counter-mobilization to the BRICS emerged at the 2012 New Delhi Summit. However, significantly, this backlash was not associated with the BRICS per se, but involved instead the proliferation of protests by Tibetan activists over the presence of Chinese President Hu Jintao at the summit. Rallies were held and one activist set himself on fire and subsequently died. Still, although these summits helped to securitize BRICS along the lines of the other informal summits, they did not alter the basic relationship between state and society concerning the operation of the summits.

It was only at the fifth summit held in 2013 at Durban, that some element of counter-mobilization was directed against the BRICS process itself. Similar to the societal forces that rose up against both the G7/8 and the G20, alternative, 'BRICS from below' protests (see Figure 8) were a contrast to the official state-based projects. Much of this counter-mobilization centred on the question of what material interests were driving the BRICS summit process, and more specifically South Africa's reasons for buying into the project. Critics who wanted fuller engagement pushed for South Africa to position itself explicitly as the 'voice' for Africa, a stance that received considerable resistance (including strong arguments from think tanks in India) on the basis that states should speak only for themselves. Critics who stayed apart from the process, for their part, vehemently expressed the concern

8. The BRICS from below. Counter summit in Durban, South Africa.

that the BRICS constituted a new type of imperialism that would carve up the resource wealth of Africa.

The 2014 Fortaleza Summit also drew protests, notably from the Homeless Workers' Movement (Movimento dos Trabalhadores Sem Teto), which blocked a major highway with burning tyres on the opening day of the summit. In addition, the summit prompted society mobilization through 'Dialogues on Development: The BRICS from the Perspective of the People', which followed the 'BRICS from below' meeting of civil society organizations held the previous year in Durban. Despite the emergence of these parallel summit processes, however, in contrast to growing cooperation at the governmental level, civil society action and resistance within the BRICS countries remains fragmented and relatively muted.

Building a networked constituency

Moves to build a broader network constituency for the BRICS beyond the state began with an outreach effort aimed at showcasing the benefits of BRICS cooperation to the business communities within the member states. Borrowing from the model established by the IBSA Dialogue Forum's Business Council, the BRICS Business Council was established at the 2013 Durban Summit with participation from twenty-five prominent entrepreneurs from Brazil, Russia, India, China, and South Africa, representing various industries and sectors.

South Africa's leadership in the initiative was particularly evident, and indicated that its business community saw benefits in a project that tied them closer to the other BRICS states in general and China in particular. The South African government appointed Patrice Motsepe, a mining magnate and major beneficiary of black empowerment deals (and incidentally the first person outside the United States to take the 'Giving Pledge', started by Microsoft founder Bill Gates and billionaire Warren Buffett, to donate half the income generated by his family assets to charity), to be the first chair of the Business Council.

The creation of the BRICS Business Council took place in the context of steady growth in intra-BRICS trade. In 2012, South Africa's total trade with its BRICS partners stood at $34.4 billion, an increase of 11 per cent on the 2011 figure of $31.9 billion. Trade with Brazil grew to $2.3 billion in 2012, up from $2.2 billion in 2011. Trade with Russia grew 45 per cent from 2011 to 2012, from $0.4 billion to $0.6 billion. And trade with India, South Africa's sixth largest trading partner, grew to $7.8 billion in 2012, from $6.4 billion in 2011, a jump of 26 per cent. While competition in manufacturing generated controversy, China made a dramatic leap to become South Africa's largest bilateral trading partner, with trade growing to $23.5 billion in 2012, up from $22.8 billion in 2011.

Since its establishment in 2013, the BRICS Council has met regularly to discuss issues related to enhancing economic ties between the member countries and to enhance dialogue between the business community and state officials. To that end, the Council has established a series of sector working groups encompassing representatives of prominent firms, and has put forward proposals and recommendations directed at both the business community and member state governments.

In their first annual report, delivered in 2014, the council outlined a number of proposals including the creation of a BRICS portal for information exchange, the establishment of special visa arrangements to encourage greater mobility between the countries, the harmonization of some technical standards, and the broader promotion of an environment conducive to trade and investment. Building on this foundation, the second annual report delivered in 2015 focused on trade in local currencies, facilitating business travel, and encouraging trade, investment, and infrastructure development.

In addition to engagement with business groups, the BRICS has witnessed an expansion of think tank activity connected to the summit process. A significant example of this growing engagement is the leadership role undertaken by the ORF, a top Indian think tank (backed by major funding from the Reliance group) in developing the NDB. This insider role was consolidated with the formal establishment of the BRICS Think Tanks Council in 2013 at Durban, with membership allocated to the China Centre for Contemporary World Studies, Russia's National Committee for BRICS Research, Brazil's Institute for Applied Economic Research, and South Africa's Human Sciences Research Council, as well as the ORF.

At the 2014 Fortaleza Summit, the Think Tanks Council delivered a set of preliminary ideas and recommendations to the leaders in a report entitled *Towards a Long-Term Strategy For the BRICS*, which focused on strengthening cooperation in the areas of economic growth and development, peace and security, social justice, sustainable development and quality of life, political and economic governance, and knowledge and innovation sharing. At the subsequent Ufa Summit in 2015, it delivered a much more detailed report elaborating challenges and national initiatives and outlining a series of recommendations in each of the five key areas.

A BRICS Trade Union Forum has also been established by trade union representatives in the five countries with the aim of developing linkages among national-level groups and elevating social and labour rights concerns. In addition, the 2014 Fortaleza Summit played host to the first Women's Forum of the BRICS Countries, which similarly sought to build links between national groups focused on women's rights. Finally, in 2015 the BRICS countries established Civic BRICS in an effort to broaden dialogue between civil society groups and member state representatives.

While these moves to broaden outreach have not, to date, fully addressed criticism of the BRICS from civil society groups, there have been wider expressions of engagement and support of the process. Trade union representatives, for example, have expressed support for the creation of the NDB as an instrument for transforming the global economic architecture. Other social activists were equally enthusiastic about the principles (if not all the operational practices) behind the NDB, in that it was deemed favourable for the advance of infrastructure and sustainable development projects including smart finance to local small and medium enterprises. For South Africa, uniquely, the NDB received kudos as a promising tool to promote local black-owned companies, especially in target sectors such as tourism and agriculture.

In issue-specific terms, encouragement for a robust anti-establishment approach to Internet governance was also evident, with the Coalition for a Just and Equitable Internet (Just Net Coalition), a civil society organization, calling for the BRICS to take the lead in creating new open Internet platforms and tools for search engines, operating systems, data storage, and cloud services. The BRICS ministers responsible for science and technology met in Cape Town for the first time in May 2014, and were urged by the Just Net Coalition to sign a memorandum of understanding that explicitly committed them to collaborate on open source secure software and communications hardware.

BRICS cooperation has also extended into the area of health. At their first meeting in July 2011 in Beijing, the BRIC health ministers met and discussed four priorities: strengthening domestic health systems, largely by developing and ensuring access to health technologies; combating the double burden of infectious and non-communicable diseases; supporting international organizations as well as global health partnerships; and promoting technology transfers to developing countries. Since their inaugural meeting the health ministers have met annually at stand-alone meetings as well as on the sidelines of the World Health Organization's annual World Health Assembly. Groups such as the Global Health Strategies initiatives (GHSi), an international non-profit organization working to increase access to health technologies and services in developing countries, have reinforced the potential buy-in by civil society with respect to the BRICS engagement in global health, pointing to the advances made by BRICS in reshaping the global development and health agenda.

Still, even with this shift towards a looser and more network-based approach to cooperation the BRICS remains a solidly state-led forum. Members of the BRICS Business Council continue to be selected by state officials. Many of the organizations brought into the BRICS Think Tanks Council are arms of the state structure, notably the China Centre for Contemporary World Studies, which publishes *Contemporary World*, a journal affiliated with the International Department of the Communist Party of China's Central Committee. As a result, growing trends towards openness and engagement in the BRICS summit process should not be overstated.

Countervailing forces: strengthening the state-centric club culture

Indeed, at odds with the logic of the need for opening up participation, in some important ways the state centrism of the BRICS has increased in recent years. A case in point is the group's growing embrace of elements of a geostrategic-oriented policy agenda, which points to the exclusion of civil society groups and broader social issues in favour of a focus on the 'high politics' of international security. While these issues were initially de-emphasized with respect to economic priorities, over time the BRICS has extended its scope of operation in two related areas.

First, it revived the foreign policy component, after a period of downplaying due to the global financial crisis. In September 2013, the first full meeting of the BRICS foreign ministers since 2010 (and the entry of South Africa) took place in New York on the sidelines of the General Assembly, followed by another gathering in March 2014 (with Russia's Sergey Lavrov, India's Salman Khurshid, China's Wang Yi, South Africa's Maite Nkoana-Mashabane, and Brazil's Alberto Figueiredo in attendance) at the Nuclear Security Summit in the Hague. No formal meeting of foreign ministers was held at the July 2014 Fortaleza Summit, although Figueiredo and Lavrov took prominent and public roles in the proceedings.

Second, the BRICS began to renew their emphasis on national security. The BRIC's national security advisers (NSAs) met on the sidelines of each summit and at a formal meeting in May 2009 to discuss the security implications of the global financial crisis.

Still, the first structured meeting with the BRICS membership only came at the 2012 New Delhi Summit. This shift indicated that the BRICS members as a group possessed a greater appetite for risk and were visibly prepared to discuss a number of tough security-related questions such as the situation in Syria and Iran as well as cyber-security. The sensitivity of this move was magnified by the fact that Dai Bingguo, China's long-serving and influential NSA, was also the lead negotiator of the contentious boundary dispute between China and India. As with the overall approach of the BRICS, nonetheless, the club culture was deeply ingrained in the workings of the NSAs, with the onus on areas of convergence.

The willingness of the BRICS to extend a unified sense of purpose to the cyber-security issue was particularly noteworthy, given that Russia, China, and Brazil had all been systematically targeted by the US National Security Agency's Prism surveillance programme. Media reports at the time of the New Delhi Summit reported that Brazil was leading an initiative to create a 'BRICS cable' that would independently link the member countries, connecting the cities of Fortaleza to Vladivostok via Cape Town, Chennai, and Shantou. While the operational feasibility of this type of project could be questioned from the start, both in terms of funding and the protection of data, a scenario along these lines presented an image of strength and solidarity rather than vulnerability in the face of collective threats.

The NSA meetings also sent a loud signal that the BRICS possessed much greater policy weight than the IBSA Dialogue Forum. This shift was confirmed by the extent of India's about-face. In 2010, before the second BRIC summit and fourth IBSA meeting, the Indian ministry of foreign affairs had pronounced that the BRIC remained 'in a nascent state' whereas the 'older grouping' (namely IBSA) remained solidly in place. Certainly its own continued prioritizing of IBSA was evident in 2011 when Singh took not only his external affairs minister, S. M. Krishna, and his minister of commerce, Anand Sharma, but also his principal secretary Pulok Chatterjee and NSA Shivshankar Menon to the fifth IBSA meeting in Pretoria. By 2012, as punctuated by the meeting of the BRICS' NSAs in 2012, this priority had changed. The BRICS was clearly on the ascendancy not only in reputational terms but also as the go-to institution on sensitive global issues.

Growing BRICS cooperation in the arena of high politics thus suggests a potential move away from enhanced engagement with civil society organizations. More broadly, the engagement of an ever greater array of state officials within the process points to a deepening of club-based participation, with more and more ministries becoming involved, but the involvement of societal groups in a network approach will be conducted in an episodic and subordinated position. As such, specific developments that point to the potential opening up of the BRICS forum are balanced against others that reinforce the state-centric character of the group.

Conclusion

Clear tensions persist between official BRICS cooperation at the governmental level and non-state actors. As a result, civil society movements in resistance to the BRICS have emerged and maintain some profile. Efforts at outreach beyond the summit level through an evolving network of think tanks have generated subsequent criticism from participants as a result of constraints imposed by state structures. Civil society groups complain about the restrictive nature of the BRICS Academic Forum and its failure to include voices beyond researchers and economists, the lack of any formal means of interaction, and the absence of any contact between BRICS leaders and civil society representatives.

Positioning themselves as potential partners, other NGOs have sought methods by which they could improve access to the BRICS.

Of particular note here is the initiative by the FIM-Forum for Democratic Global Governance to replicate its efforts on the G7/8-G20 to launch the Civil Society–BRICS Engagement Initiative in November 2011. Although the project was housed within FIM, there was active participation in this effort by India's PRIA (Participatory Research in Asia), Brazil's Instituto Pólis, South Africa's Isandla Institute, the China Participation Centre, and the Commission on Social Policies, Labour and Living Standards of the Civic Chamber of the Russian Federation.

Incentives will likely build to create a broad network of non-state actors among the five countries, although the BRICS will surely retain the essence of its club culture. The main force driving this balance between the states and civil society will be the desire to enhance efficiency, as BRICS officials will inevitably require expertise outside government to deliver their expanded agenda. The spectacle of the BRICS should push similar outcomes. As with the G7 and G20 summits, BRICS leaders' forums risk a loss of attention if their agenda is too narrowly constituted. The organizational profile of the BRICS needs to widen, in the sense that a summit moves from being a hub for leaders' interaction to a focal point for wider debate and policy direction. Engagement with diverse domestic publics, although messy, can create movement along this path. For sure, there are some indications of the BRICS moving away from a state-centric model. One interesting illustration is the proliferation of meetings on the theme of sustainable urbanization, through the BRICS urbanization forums, meetings of friendship cities, and local government cooperation forums.

Reduced to its core dimension, therefore, the BRICS remains a highly political state-based project. Whatever the framework used, its evolution underscores the fact that the members have upgraded their image on the global stage, and deserve respect for doing so. Such a process of status enhancement is consistent with the trajectory of other countries seeking recognition in earlier eras. That being said, the unique style of the BRICS as a forum with an embedded club culture attenuates the image of history repeating itself. The pattern of the sustained collectivity of the BRICS, unlike rising powers in the past, showcases informality and improvisation over formal binding modes of operation. Although the state centric orientation remains strong, the opportunity has opened up to increase the diversity of participation as the BRICS moves forward.

Chapter 7
The staying power of the BRICS

The BRICS possesses multiple identities, each of which is strong enough to merit a specific analysis. The image of the cluster of big emerging economies with dramatic growth jump-started the conceptual invention of the label. The utilization of the acronym BRIC or BRICS, which downplays any club and geostrategic implications, has been one of the massive material assets fuelling the group's rise. Favoured by an impressively confident cluster of consultants and investment banks, such an interpretation privileges an individual but disaggregated ascendancy without paying attention to the features that separate the individual countries.

In juxtaposition to this economic-driven narrative, the BRICS viewed as an international institution highlights its transition from an artificial entity into actual diplomatic modes of operation. Whereas the concept developed in the form of BRIC by Goldman Sachs serves as a marketing tool to showcase the investment opportunities available in China, India, Brazil, and Russia, the state-based model provides a means by which a cluster of ascendant states could raise their degree of recognition in the global system. The concept of the BRICS as big emerging economies is tied inexorably with commercial opportunities. In contradistinction, the framing of the BRICS as a forum with an embedded club culture focuses on status enhancement.

Privileging the BRICS as a potential alliance, in turn, shifts the focus to the geostrategic arena. In this highly contested interpretation, the BRICS explicitly challenges the old Western establishment. According to classic international relations theory, this analysis views the group neither as a cluster of disaggregated big emerging economies nor as a diplomatic club of reform-minded members seeking a new and fairer deal in the world's institutional architecture. Rather, it regards the BRICS as having the troublesome potential to cause a rupture in the global system.

While the mix of these three divergent interpretations puts the BRICS into the spotlight, the absence of a single dominant identity accentuates the need for a broad overview. If the BRICS is examined only through one of these lenses, its nature and meaning can be either diminished to a level of abstract meaninglessness or overblown beyond practical limits.

In terms of economic profiles, the interpretation of the BRICS as a cluster of big, dynamic entities has become most analytically problematic. When the BRIC model was formulated in 2001 by Goldman Sachs, Brazil, Russia, India, and China were placed in a top-tier league of their own, deemed to be moving higher and faster in their material trajectory than any other possible cluster. Although other groups—including Goldman Sachs' own N11—had enormous potential as growth centres, they were profiled as up and coming, rather than in the top tier akin with the BRIC countries.

Over time, however, this distinction between the BRIC or BRICS and other clusters looks overblown. Objectively, the rationale for positioning those countries in a distinctive category of super elite entities seems less compelling. The momentum of economic growth has ebbed considerably, with the image of BRICS as a special class as showcased in the original Goldman Sachs concept weakening appreciably.

As *The Economist* cartoon highlights (see Figure 9), only China has maintained the projections anticipated by Goldman Sachs. Even Chinese growth slowed down on the basis of official figures to 7.5 per cent in 2013 and 7.4 per cent in 2014, a slowdown exacerbated by severe stock market volatility in 2015. In a not so subtle rebuke, Morgan Stanley—a rival firm to Goldman Sachs—situated Brazil, India, and South Africa as part of a new 'fragile five' category, along with Turkey and Indonesia.

Not only do the BRICS members disappoint in terms of their economic projections, but other indicators of comparative performance that were downplayed by Goldman Sachs have gained prominence in public policy debates. With rising expectations about economic growth come other forms of aspirational demands, such as expanded social services and personal safety. The image of ascendant status on a state-centric basis is disconnected from the image of societal limitations at the national level.

Under these changing conditions, the BRICS as a branding tool has lost a considerable degree of its attractiveness. The depiction of some of the BRICS countries as underperforming—not overperforming as in the original depiction—has been exacerbated by the inclination of consultants and investment bankers to keep looking for the next big thing beyond the BRICS. Although the BRICS countries may have lost their robustness as comparative growth stories, an air of excitement animated positive narratives about the growth of other emerging economies. Jim O'Neill's self-distancing from the concept added to this image of decline. As early as 2011, he appeared far more impressed by the economic prospects of Mexico, Korea, Turkey, and Indonesia than by the BRIC countries. Only China—the massive 'C' in BRIC—escaped his disappointment in the trajectory of the original cluster, the promise of which he had enthused about in 2001.

Notwithstanding this backlash from the investment banking community, the original BRICs continue to exist in a league

9. 'The Great Deceleration'. This cartoon from the 27 July 2013 issue of *The Economist* illustrates the economic slowdown among the four biggest BRICS members, led by China.

completely separate from the countries put together in competitive acronyms such as MIST, MINT, or CIVETS. In terms of measurable criteria, the gap comes out clearly in terms of nominal GDP. As compiled by the IMF, the comparative data for 2013 put China's economy at $9,469 billion, highest among the BRICS members, followed by Brazil at $2,391 billion, Russia at

$2,079 billion, and India at $1,875 billion, with South Africa down the list at $366 billion. By way of comparison, the cluster of significant non-BRICS (Mexico, Korea, Indonesia, and Turkey) lagged behind all but South Africa: Korea's nominal GDP for 2013 is $1,304 billion, Mexico's is $1,262 billion, Indonesia's is $912 billion, and Turkey's is $821 billion.

Politically, the contrast between the BRICS and non-BRICS put together in various labelling exercises reflects the different levels of recognition given to the latter type of non-Western countries by the old Western establishment. Korea, Mexico, Turkey, and Indonesia have gained membership in the G20, but aside from Mexico were never considered for G8 membership in an expanded summit process. Nor, unlike China, India, Brazil, and South Africa (as the representative of Africa), were they deemed systemically important. Indeed, these countries were only included in the G20 at the discretion of the United States, which saw political advantages from a diluted BRICS-plus approach.

The second frame showcasing the distinctive diplomatic personality of the BRICS also has serious limitations. While the existence of a strong club culture is vital for understanding how the BRICS has stayed together, notwithstanding all the members' differences, this interpretation points to the boundaries of collective operation. BRICS members may be able to agree about what not to do, but have found it much harder to agree about constructive activity. The concentration on the unfairness of representation in the IFIs, above all, has not translated into a coherent resolution of this problem.

Nor has there been a consistency of purpose in other areas of collective action. At the height of the euro crisis, the idea of a joint BRICS initiative with respect to a European bailout was mooted by the Brazilian finance minister Guido Mantega. Yet no concerted effort could be mobilized. At the G20's 2011 Cannes Summit, China displayed little enthusiasm for this type of ambitious initiative, offering only that the BRICS create a consultative mechanism to watch the European situation closely and exchange ideas on relevant issues and strengthened coordination. India stated that in principle it was ready to stem any contagion effect, but in practice backed away from any such move, saying that it had not received any firm request for help. South Africa, for its part, did not see the BRICS as a lead actor in any rescue move. Indeed, given the size of its own economy, South Africa could not play anything akin to a substantive role in moving the eurozone out of its debt crisis.

It was only at the G20 Los Cabos Summit in June 2012 that the BRICS countries were able to mount any form of collective effort, with the infusion of substantial funds into the IMF's extended firewall, with China committing $43 billion, Brazil, Russia, and India pledging $10 billion, and South Africa offering $2 billion. This commitment, nonetheless, came with some measure of conditionality, with these resources only called upon after existing resources were utilized—and under condition that IFI reform be implemented.

Still, for all these limitations, BRICS members have consolidated their relationship in a manner that belies predictions that the group would fade away. Goldman Sachs conceptualized the BRIC in 2001 as dynamic economies that shared certain economic features but were not connected by any sense of complex interdependence. For more than a decade, this forging of interdependence among the five countries has been the dominant feature. Although with much space to grow (intra-BRICS trade is still only approximately 10 per cent of members' combined trade), in 2012 trade between Brazil, Russia, India, China, and South Africa reached $276 billion, up from $27 billion in 2002. In large part this pattern of extended ties was a testimony to the massive role of China, in that it is the only member to have impressive economic ties with all of the other members. It has moved into the lead in terms of trade with

Brazil, India, and South Africa, while retaining the number two position vis-à-vis Russia.

However, there are signs that the BRICS relationship has catalysed deal-making beyond arrangements involving China. One such arrangement that has attracted considerable attention is negotiations for Russia's atomic energy agency to provide up to eight nuclear reactors to South Africa by 2023.

Another indicator of the sustained nature comes from the elaboration and refinement of the group's club diplomacy. While maintaining its informality, with no legal personality and no fixed schedule of summits, secretariat, or hierarchy, the BRICS has been notably able to sustain itself in terms of group dynamics. Even under conditions of acute stress, as problematic financial pressure points tilted away from the old Western establishment to the new BRICS members themselves, and with the tapering policy of the US Federal Reserve, the BRICS has maintained a sense of solidarity in meetings, such as its mini-summits held just before the G20 summits at Cannes in 2012, St Petersburg in 2013, and Brisbane in 2014. At the declaratory level, the BRICS issued a collective call for the United States to be sensitive to the global implications of its move to unwind monetary stimulus. Operationally, the BRICS ramped up its collective attempt to protect its members from the impact of these external turbulent forces and created a $100 billion reserve fund for currency swap arrangements among the five countries.

Such reactions were not produced without cost, but strikingly this cost was deflected elsewhere. Indeed, the biggest casualty of BRICS consolidation has been the IBSA Dialogue Forum, the alternative body set up by India, Brazil, and South Africa at the leaders' level before the initial BRICS summit. With a separate identity that underscored the vibrant democratic credentials of these three countries, along with their robust private sector and civil society participation, IBSA retained some comparative advantage in terms of global identity. In operational practice, however, it was crowded out by the animation of the wider summit process that included China and Russia. In 2013, India postponed the IBSA Dialogue Forum at the leaders' level, and future plans for a revival remain speculative.

The third, and final, frame turns from complex interdependence and low-key diplomacy to the image of the BRICS as an explicit challenger to the existing global system. Instead of identifying a pattern of engagement, this scenario points to heightened polarization between the old Western establishment and the new BRICS extending into the security sphere. It views the BRICS as deeply dissatisfied not only with the international architecture but also with the normative pillars underpinning the system, rather than as actors with a massive stake in the established system, albeit ones that want reforms to even the institutional playing field.

From this perspective, the BRICS are reluctant participants in institution building, or, put more colloquially by former Mexican foreign minister Jorge Castañeda, they are not yet ready for 'prime time'. This criticism has some truth in it, in that the BRICS has rarely put any of its own initiatives up for consideration in hub forums such as the G20. Leaving policy entrepreneurship to others, the BRICS remains stuck in a reactive and defensive mindset.

In the context of gaining autonomous ownership of their own forum, however, the BRICS members are increasingly able to take initiatives in terms of both convening and setting the agenda. Here the prime illustration is the initiative on the establishment of the NDB, an idea that managed to emerge despite the persistence of deep-seated rivalry among the BRICS countries. The diplomacy involved in the 2014 Fortaleza Summit on this issue stood out for its skill and sensitivity about distributive outcomes. By the time of the Ufa Summit, therefore, the NDB had officially commenced operation with the prospect that the first projects to finance would be selected by April 2016.

Another far more problematic interpretation of the BRICS is that its members can—and do—act (to use the phrase by Stewart Patrick from the US Council on Foreign Relations) as 'irresponsible stakeholders' within the global system. To put their own interests and identity first, the BRICS countries push back at the Western establishment on a number of security-related issues. At the 2010 Brasilia Summit, host Luiz Inácio Lula da Silva mobilized a counter-response to the West's imposition of sanctions against Iran. At the 2011 Sanya Summit, the leaders—including South Africa's Jacob Zuma—criticized the North Atlantic Treaty Organization's air strikes against Libya. At the 2012 New Delhi Summit the target of concern was the prospect of Western military intervention with respect to Syria.

The difference between the contestation in the context of these earlier meetings and the controversy that arose at the 2014 and 2015 summits was the focal point of the issue in question. At the earlier forums, the BRICS focused on external issues, that is to say, questions dealing with Iran, Libya, and Syria in which the members took a stance but were not directly involved as participants. At the 2014 Fortaleza and 2015 Ufa Summits, in contradistinction, the focus turned towards the Crimea/Ukraine crisis, inextricably involving Russia. As such, the stakes for BRICS have risen appreciably. Given Russia's exclusion from the G8, the BRICS took on a greater importance as a vehicle by which Russia could project its interests—a situation magnified by Russia's hosting of the 2015 summit at Ufa. In the March 2014 issue of *Foreign Policy*, Suzanne Nossel, a former deputy assistant secretary of state for the Bureau of International Organization Affairs under the Obama administration, asked whether 'Putin will either be left friendless or will succeed in turning the BRICS, a coalition of Brazil, Russia, India, China, and South Africa, into a tight new clique'.

There was some supporting evidence for the idea that Russia is indeed using the BRICS to build an anti-Western constellation of forces. Geostrategically, Vladimir Putin's pre-summit tour on the way to Fortaleza held strong counter-hegemonic overtones, with a symbolic meeting with Russia's old ally Fidel Castro in Havana, as well as moves to consolidate relations with Venezuela's Nicolás Maduro and Bolivia's Evo Morales along with Uruguay's José 'Pepe' Mujica (with the meeting with Mujica opening up the sensitive question of support for the construction of a deep-water port).

The geopolitical dimensions of BRICS were even more apparent at the 2015 Ufa Summit. Not only did the other BRICS go along with the Russian strategy of merging the BRICS summit with the summit of the SCO, together with an informal meeting of the Eurasian Economic Union (with only Russia a member of all three organizations), there was no push back on the move by President Putin to allow President Hassan Rouhani 'special guest' status at both the BRICS and SCO summits subsequent to Russian–Iranian bilateral meetings that included discussions on military-technological cooperation, in particular, an exchange in missions of naval ships.

Still, to suggest that the BRICS possesses a different identity and range of interests from the West is not the same as saying that the BRICS is becoming an anti-West alliance powered by Russia. As in the case of the response by the BRICS to the suggestion by Australian foreign minister Julie Bishop that Russia would be excluded from the G20's Brisbane Summit in November 2014, the prime rationale for the BRICS in the context of Ukraine is to keep Russia from becoming isolated within the global system.

In a rebuke to the Australian G20 proposal for denying Russian participation, the BRICS foreign ministers issued a statement that 'the custodianship of the G20 belongs to all Member States equally and no one Member State can unilaterally determine its nature or character'. On the issue of Ukraine, the concern of the BRICS is not to subject President Putin to any public rebuke. At Fortaleza the BRICS maintained its generalized opposition to unilateral action, with the view that 'no State should strengthen its security at the expense of the security of others'. In keeping with the embedded club culture, at Ufa as in Fortaleza, the leaders did not refer specifically to Russia's actions but only to the BRICS' 'deep concern about the situation in Ukraine' and the need to resolve the situation through 'inclusive political dialogue'.

This mode of operation also deflected attention away from the question of whether the BRICS is a closed club, with a fixed membership, or whether it should or could expand. The importance of this question was initially raised by the relationship of Argentina to the BRICS, with Russia inviting the president of Argentina, Cristina Fernández de Kirchner, to the Fortaleza Summit amid conjecture in Buenos Aires that the name of the group could possibly be changed to BRICSA. Such a scenario was given some encouragement, moreover, by the high-profile visit of China's President Xi Jinping to Argentina (with the signing of a number of infrastructure deals and an upgrading of the relationship to 'an integrated strategic association'), as part of his own tour that also included Cuba and Venezuela.

Again, though, the priority on organizational maintenance held up. Notwithstanding speculation about the process of enlargement, the BRICS maintained the status quo. Although he briefly visited Argentina, after the summit Putin said that the BRICS had no immediate plans to expand as a group. And to reinforce this point, Brazilian president Dilma Rousseff made it clear that Argentina was not a founding member of the NDB, and that it could only be entitled to monies from the emergency reserve fund if it made a formal request.

A similar scenario played out with respect to Greece and the NDB. Speculation mounted prior to the Ufa Summit of a Russian

invitation for Greece to become the sixth member of the bank.
Yet, although in his press conference following the summit
Putin extolled Russia's 'special relationship' with Greece,
he commented that the 'figures are too high' for any offer of
assistance to be made.

A scenario of increasing tensions between the West and the
BRICS is possible but not probable. Russia has an incentive to
push the BRICS towards a more confrontational position, but the
other BRICS members do not support this approach. The global
system continues to offer them massive benefits. In any case, if the
BRICS intended to cause a rupture, the global financial crisis
provided an opportunity to do so. But, rather than decisively
separating themselves from the old establishment, the BRICS
countries have hedged their bets by operating in a fashion that
allows them to participate as insiders in the G20 and outsiders
with a stand-alone forum of their own.

Such hedging can be considered as a sign of incompleteness,
with the BRICS taken to be a mix of its parts rather than
something whole and coherent. However, in institutional terms
it is precisely this flexibility that provides the BRICS with its
staying power. Pushed into the spotlight by the size and
dynamism of their economies, the BRICS members have
maintained their leverage by sending a message to the old
Western establishment that the rules of the game in the
21st century have changed. Buttressed by the data from
Goldman Sachs and a shared sense of triumphalism, the BRICS
could demonstrate that it is too big to ignore: not because of
equality resting on a normative foundation of fairness but
because of its members' sheer economic weight and leverage.

The BRICS could also signal, through its diplomatic club culture,
that it is willing to work from within to reform the international
system, even though it has other options in its repertoire. For all of
their differences, each member benefits from the establishment of

an informal institution of their own. China has avoided the risk of isolation, magnified by the fast-moving pace of its ascendancy. Russia, by way of contrast, has used the BRICS to compensate for its decline. Faced with so many dilemmas in terms of their socio-political environments, India, Brazil, and South Africa use the BRICS to gain leverage through an alternative collective identity.

However, the impact of the BRICS on the inner political workings of its members should not be exaggerated. The BRICS has not taken a prominent role with respect to the election process in Brazil, India, or South Africa. Nor does it intrude into core bilateral issues, for example, the shift in relations between India and the United States after the election of Narendra Modi, or the nature of the strategic dialogue between the United States and China. Each member displays its BRICS identity as a primary reference point only intermittently.

It is precisely this looseness in form that bestows staying power on the BRICS. Underneath the surface, there have been all sorts of internal disputes—on the membership of South Africa, the role South Africa should play with respect to the rest of Africa, on the response to the euro crisis, the relationship of BRICS to IBSA, the role of non-state actors, and the construction of the NDB. Such differences could have torn the group apart. Yet, through all of these severe tests to the sustainability of club culture, the BRICS members have not only stuck together, but have become far more entangled in a wider and deeper set of activities.

Ultimately, the BRICS deserves credit for skilfully navigating its transition from abstract conceptualization to operational take-off, and for ramping up collective action without systemic dislocation. Its success in making this transition points to the role of the BRICS in showcasing a fundamental, albeit still awkward and incomplete, shift in the global system. In doing so, its consolidated existence and performance refutes any counter-interpretation that the old Western establishment can continue to manage the system on a narrowly constructed basis. Although the transformative effect of the BRICS can be overblown, both its symbolic and operational role in the diffusion of authority in the 21st-century global system should not be underestimated.

References

Chapter 1: Framing the BRICS

The declaration that 'a new global economic geography has been born' is from Luiz Inácio Lula da Silva, 'At Yekaterinburg, the BRICs come of age', *The Hindu*, 16 June 2009. The article is available from <http://www.thehindu.com/todays-paper/tp-opinion/at-yekaterinburg-the-brics-come-of-age/article261939.ece>.

Vladimir Putin's view that BRICS will turn into 'a full-scale strategic management system' is quoted in 'BRICS key element of emerging multipolar world—Putin', *Russia Today*, 22 March 2013. This article is available from <http://rt.com/news/brics-multipolar-world-putin-635/>.

Chapter 2: A contested invention

The prediction that 'China, together with emerging Asia, stands a very good chance of decoupling from the US economy in the coming few years' is from Hong Liang, 'Asia economics flash', Goldman Sachs Economic Research, 29 November 2008. This paper is available from <http://www.ghsl.cn/insight/case_studies/pdf/our_growth_and_inflation_outlook_for_2008_and_2009.pdf>.

Nicolas Sarkozy's support for an expansion of the G8 is in 'French prez wants India in G8', *The Times of India*, 31 August 2007. This article is available from <http://timesofindia.indiatimes.com/India/French_prez_wants_India_in_G8/rssarticleshow/2324874.cms>.

Manmohan Singh's critical remarks about the Heiligendamm Process were widely circulated in the Indian media. For one example see Narayanan Madhavan, 'G8 glass ceiling upsets India', *Hindustan Times*, 11 June 2007 at <http://www.hindustantimes.com/newdelhi/g8-glass-ceiling-upsets-india/article1-229141.aspx>.

China's view that the outreach process should not be used as a means for exerting leverage is asserted by assistant foreign minister Cui Tiankai. His comments are available in Chen Feng, 'G8 not platform for exerting pressure', *Xinhua*, 4 June 2007, <http://www.gov.cn/misc/2007-06/04/content_636224.htm>.

The first unofficial meeting of BRIC leaders was held at the end of the G8 summit in Toyako, Japan, in July 2008. Reference to the meeting is in 'The leaders of the BRIC countries (Brazil, Russia, India and China) met during the G8 summit in Japan', Kremlin, 9 July 2008, available at <http://archive.kremlin.ru/eng/text/news/2008/07/203929.shtml>.

Lula's use of statistics to buttress the position of the BRIC countries is provided in Luiz Inácio Lula da Silva, 'At Yekaterinburg, the BRICs come of age', *The Hindu*, 16 June 2009. The article is available from <http://www.thehindu.com/todays-paper/tp-opinion/at-yekaterinburg-the-brics-come-of-age/article261939.ece>.

Chapter 3: A historical departure

Marius Fransman's reference to the legacy of Bandung for the BRICS is made in a public lecture on the theme 'South Africa: a strong African brick in BRICS', at Stellenbosch University on 21 November 2012. The address is available from <http://www.polity.org.za/article/sa-marius-fransman-address-by-the-deputy-minister-of-of-international-relations-and-cooperation-during-a-public-lecture-on-on-the-theme-south-africa-a-strong-african-brick-in-brics-stellenbosch-21112012-2012-11-21>.

Chapter 4: Hanging together

Nikolas Gvosdev, 'The realist prism: what the U.S. can learn from the BRICS', *World Politics Review*, 22 June 2012. This article is available from <http://www.worldpoliticsreview.com/articles/12087/the-realist-prism-what-the-u-s-can-learn-from-the-brics>.

Wen Jiabao's criticism of the West's financial exuberance and mismanagement is from a speech at the annual World Economic Forum meeting on 28 January 2009. The full text of this speech is provided at <http://news.xinhuanet.com/english/2009-01/29/content_10731877.htm>.

Murli Deora's criticism of the Western-centric nature of the financial crisis is contained in a speech he made in Beijing. The text is available from the Press Information Bureau of the Government of India, 'SCO has important role in dealing with global financial crisis; time for zero tolerance to terrorism', 14 October 2009, at <http://pib.nic.in/newsite/erelcontent.aspx?relid=53185>.

Hu Jintao elaborated on the importance of the BRICS before attending the fourth BRICS Summit. His comments are available in 'BRICS is the defender of the developing world', *The Hindu*, 28 March 2012, at <http://www.thehindu.com/todays-paper/tp-opinion/brics-is-the-defender-of-the-developing-world/article3252370.ece>.

Dilma Rousseff's view that Brazil and India strongly converged on the need for reform of international organizations is expressed in 'We're all in it together', *Times of India*, 29 March 2012. The text of this commentary is available from <http://articles.timesofindia.indiatimes.com/2012-03-29/edit-page/31250213_1_brics-brazil-countries>.

The ambiguity of the BRIC countries on reform of the United Nations is expressed in the 'Joint communiqué of the meeting of Celso Amorim, Minister of Foreign Relations of Brazil, Sergei Lavrov, Minister of Foreign Affairs of the Russian Federation, Pranab Mukherjee, Minister of External Affairs of the Republic of India, and Yang Jechi, Minister of Foreign Affairs of the People's Republic of China', issued at Yekaterinburg, Russia, on 16 May 2008. The text is available from <http://www.brics.utoronto.ca/docs/080516-foreign.html>.

The call for reform of the IFIs is from the 2011 Sanya Declaration of the BRICS Leaders Meeting, 14 April 2011. The full text is available from <http://www.brics.utoronto.ca/docs/110414-leaders.html>.

The criticism by the BRICS members of the deleterious policy actions by the United States and the European Union is expressed in the Fourth BRICS Summit—Delhi Declaration, 29 March 2012. The text is available from <http://www.brics.utoronto.ca/docs/120329-delhi-declaration.html>.

Chapter 5: Building the New Development Bank

The proposal for the establishment of a development bank is included in the recommendations of the 2012 BRICS Academic Forum, Delhi, 6 March 2012. The text is available from <http://www.brics.utoronto.ca/docs/120306-academic-forum.html>.

China's initial attitude to the development bank is expressed by Xu Qinghong in Ananth Krishnan, 'China's caution may slow BRICS bank plan', *The Hindu*, 11 October 2011. The text is available from <http://www.thehindu.com/todays-paper/tp-business/chinas-caution-may-slow-brics-bank-plan/article3986248.ece>.

The critical comments of Lamido Sanusi about China as a major contributor to the deindustrialization of Africa are asserted in an interview with the *Financial Times*, 11 March 2013. The text is available from <http://www.ft.com/intl/cms/s/0/58b08eb0-8a6c-11e2-9da4-00144feabdc0.html#axzz3Zk2ia2gj>.

The letter by Mattia Romani, Nicholas Stern, and Joseph Stiglitz, endorsing the development bank was published in the *Financial Times* on 5 April 2012. The text is available from <http://www.ft.com/intl/cms/s/0/1770f242-7d88-11e1-81a5-00144feab49a.html#axzz3Zk2ia2gj>.

The concern by Xu Qinghong about non-economic factors as an obstacle to the creation of the NDB is expressed in an interview, 'China's caution may slow BRICS bank plan', *The Hindu*, 1 October 2011. The text is available from <http://www.thehindu.com/todays-paper/tp-business/chinas-caution-may-slow-brics-bank-plan/article3986248.ece>.

Manmohan Singh's support for the NDB as a mechanism to recycle surplus savings into infrastructure investments in developing countries is given in the 'Prime Minister's statement to the media after the Plenary Session of the 5th BRICS Summit', 27 March 2013. The text is available at <http://pib.nic.in/newsite/erelease.aspx?relid=94316>.

The support of the Financial Research Center at Fudan University for China to host the headquarters of the NDB is provided in a paper titled 'Will the BRICS Development Bank settle in Shanghai?, available in *China Watch*, 2013, pages 63–5, at <http://www.shanghaiforum.fudan.edu.cn/index.php?c=publication&a=list&typeid=10027>.

Anton Siluanov's comments about the attractions of Shanghai as the headquarters for the NDB is given in Raymond Colitt, 'Brics nations to host bank headquarters in Shanghai', *Business Day*, 18 July 2014. The text is available at <http://www.bdlive.co.za/

economy/2014/07/17/brics-nations-to-host-bank-headquarters-in-shanghai>.

The Brazilian diplomat's comment about the agreement on the NDB is quoted in Alonso Soto and Anthony Boadle, 'BRICS set up bank to counter Western hold on global finance', *Reuters*, 15 July 2014. The text is available at <http://www.reuters.com/article/2014/07/15/us-brics-summit-bank-idUSKBN0FK08V20140715>.

Dilma Rousseff's continued support for the IMF is quoted in Raymond Colitt, Unni Krishnan, and Arnaldo Galvao, 'BRICS ink $50 billion lender in World Bank, IMF challenge', *Bloomberg Business*, 16 July 2014 available at <http://www.bloomberg.com/news/articles/2014-07-16/brics-to-form-50-billion-lender-in-challenge-to-world-bank-imf>.

Elvira Nabiullina's comments about the desire of the BRICS to reach speedy practical results on the NDB is quoted in Anna Yukhananov, 'Russia says AIIB complement to BRICS bank, not replacement', *Reuters*, 16 April 2015. The text is available at <http://www.reuters.com/article/2015/04/16/us-imf-g20-brics-idUSKBN0N72W520150416>.

Xi Jinping's view that the BRICS overall commonalities trumps specific tensions is in 'President Xi's joint written interview with media from four Latin American and Caribbean countries', 15 July 2014, available at <http://news.xinhuanet.com/english/china/2014-07/15/c_126752293.htm>.

Takehiko Nakao's comments about the difficulty of setting up the NDB is in 'Setting up BRICS bank not going to be easy: Takehiko Nakao', *Economic Times*, 3 May 2013. The text is available at <http://articles.economictimes.indiatimes.com/2013-05-03/news/39009243_1_brics-countries-development-bank-sustainable-development-projects>.

The view of the Brazilian activists about the absence of the poor in the BRICS is in Pascal Fletcher, 'BRICS chafe under charge of "new imperialists" in Africa', *Reuters*, 26 March 2013. The full text is available at <http://www.reuters.com/article/2013/03/26/us-brics-africa-idUSBRE92P0FU20130326>.

Chapter 6: BRICS as the recognition of states, not societies

David Held's optimism about the G20 is in his book *Cosmopolitanism: Ideals, Realities, and Deficiencies* (Cambridge: Polity Press, 2010), page 204.

The declaratory statement of the foreign ministers for building a more democratic international system founded on the rule of law and multilateral diplomacy is from the 'Joint communiqué of the Meeting of Celso Amorim, Minister of Foreign Relations of Brazil, Sergei Lavrov, Minister of Foreign Affairs of the Russian Federation, Pranab Mukherjee, Minister of External Affairs of the Republic of India, and Yang Jechi, Minister of Foreign Affairs of the People's Republic of China', Yekaterinburg, 16 May 2006. The text is available from <http://www.brics.utoronto.ca/docs/080516-foreign.html>.

Guido Mantega's proposed updating of the 1944 Bretton Woods model is in an interview, 'BRIC want financial system overhaul', *Economic Times*, 8 November 2008. The full text is available at <http://articles.economictimes.indiatimes.com/2008-11-08/news/28461880_1_bric-countries-joint-statement-economy-minister-guido-mantega>.

The declaration of the formative meeting of the BRIC finance ministers is provided in the 'Brazil, Russia, India and China finance ministers joint communiqué' issued in São Paulo, 7 November 2008. The full text is available in <http://www.brics.utoronto.ca/docs/081107-finance.html>.

The declaration of the Horsham meeting of the BRIC finance ministers is provided in 'BRIC finance communiqué', 14 March 2009. The full text is available at <http://www.brics.utoronto.ca/docs/090314-finance.html>.

The call by the G20 leaders for IFI reform is included in the 'Global plan for recovery and reform', London, 2 April 2009. The full text is available at <http://www.g20.utoronto.ca/2009/2009communique0402.html>.

The debate in India between BRICS and the IBSA Dialogue Forum is spelled out in Rajiv Bhatia, 'BRICS set to outshine IBSA?', *The Hindu*, 30 April 2011. The full text is available at <http://www.thehindu.com/todays-paper/tp-opinion/brics-set-to-outshine-ibsa/article1979792.ece>.

Chapter 7: The staying power of the BRICS

The comparative data on gross domestic product is taken from the IMF's April 2015 World Economic Outlook Database available at <http://www.imf.org/external/pubs/ft/weo/2015/01/weodata/index.aspx>.

Jorge Castañeda's criticism of the BRICS as not being ready for prime time is in his article 'Not ready for prime time: why including emerging powers at the helm would hurt global governance', *Foreign Affairs*, September/October 2010, pages 109–22. The article is available at <https://www.foreignaffairs.com/articles/south-africa/2010-09-01/not-ready-prime-time>.

Stewart Patrick's view of BRICS as 'irresponsible stakeholders' within the global system is from his article 'Irresponsible stakeholders? The difficulty of integrating rising powers', *Foreign Affairs*, November/December 2010, pages 44–53. The article is available at <https://www.foreignaffairs.com/articles/south-africa/2010-11-01/irresponsible-stakeholders>.

Suzanne Nossel's view that BRICS poses a potential geostrategic threat is in her article 'The triumph of Putin is when good countries do nothing', *Foreign Policy*, 27 March 2014. The article is available at <http://foreignpolicy.com/2014/03/28/the-triumph-of-putin-is-when-good-countries-do-nothing/>.

The statement of the BRICS foreign ministers that the custodianship of the G20 belongs to all member states equally is from 'BRICS ministers meet on the sidelines of the Nuclear Security Summit in the Hague', 24 March 2014, The Hague. The full text is available at <http://www.brics.utoronto.ca/docs/140324-hague.html>.

The statement concerning the BRICS' 'deep concern about the situation in Ukraine' and the need to resolve the situation through 'inclusive political dialogue' is from the 2015 Ufa Declaration, 9 July 2015. The full text is available at <http://www.brics.utoronto.ca/docs/150709-ufa-declaration_en.html>.

Vladimir Putin's comments that although Russia possessed a 'special relationship' with Greece the 'figures are too high' for any offer of assistance to be made is from 'News conference by Vladimir Putin following the BRICS and Shanghai Cooperation Organization Summits in Ufa', 12 July 2015. The full text is available at <http://russia-insider.com/en/news-conference-vladimir-putin-following-brics-and-shanghai-cooperative-summits/ri8665>.

Further reading

Chapter 1: Framing the BRICS

The fullest exploration of the BRICs concept by Goldman Sachs is provided by Dominic Wilson and Roopa Purushothaman, *Dreaming with BRICs: The Path to 2050* (Global Economics Paper No. 99. Goldman Sachs, 2003). A more critical assessment is provided by Leslie Elliott Armijo, 'The BRICS countries (Brazil, Russia, India, and China) as analytical category: mirage or insight?' *Asian Perspective* (2007), vol. 31, no. 4, pp. 7–42.

On earlier alternative designs for ascendant states, see, for example, Jeffrey E. Garten, *The Big Ten: The Big Emerging Markets and How They Will Change Our Lives* (New York: Basic Books, 1997). See also Elaine Moore, 'Civets, Brics and the Next 11', *Financial Times*, 8 June 2012, available at <http://www.ft.com/intl/cms/s/0/c14730ae-aff3-11e1-ad0b-00144feabdc0.html>.

For excellent analyses of the context for the ascendancy of states from the non-West, see Andrew Hurrell, 'Hegemony, liberalism and global order: what space for would-be great powers?' *International Affairs* (2006), vol. 82, no. 1, pp. 1–19, and Paola Subacchi, 'New power centres and new power brokers: are they shaping a new economic order?' *International Affairs* (2008), vol. 84, no. 3, pp. 485–98.

For those wishing to explore the debate about the future of the global system, see G. John Ikenberry, 'The future of the liberal world order', *Foreign Affairs* (May/June 2011), vol. 90, no. 3, pp. 56–68, available at <http://www.foreignaffairs.com/articles/67730/g-john-ikenberry/the-future-of-the-liberal-world-order>, and

Charles Kupchan, *No One's World: The West, The Rising Rest, and the Coming Global Turn* (New York: Oxford University Press, 2012).

In terms of pessimistic views of the implications of China, if not the BRICS per se, see John J. Mearsheimer, 'China's unpeaceful rise', *Current History* (April 2006), vol. 106, no. 690, pp. 160–2. See also Randall Schweller, 'Emerging powers in an age of disorder', *Global Governance* (2011), vol. 17, no. 3, pp. 285–97.

On the wider constellation of forces from the global South, see Fareed Zakaria, *The Post-American World: And the Rise of the Rest* (New York: W. W. Norton, 2009).

'Joint statement of the BRIC countries' leaders', the communiqué from the first BRIC summit at the leaders' level on 16 June 2009, is available at <http://www.brics.utoronto.ca/docs/090616-leaders.html>.

For a range of informative BRICS-related websites see

Post-Western World: <http://www.postwesternworld.com>.

The BRICS Post: <http://thebricspost.com>.

BRICS Information Centre: <http://www.brics.utoronto.ca>.

Global Sherpa: <http://www.globalsherpa.org>.

Rising BRICSAM: <http://blog.risingbricsam.com>.

Center for BRICS Studies: <http://fddi.fudan.edu.cn/en/index.php?c=intro&a=show&aid=62>.

BRICS Policy Center: <http://bricspolicycenter.org>.

Russia Beyond the Headlines: <http://rbth.com/bric>.

Observer Research Foundation: <http://orfonline.org>.

Chapter 2: A contested invention

Jim O'Neill's original 2001 contribution is *Building Better Economic BRICs* (Global Economics Paper No. 66, Goldman Sachs, 2001), available at <http://www.goldmansachs.com/our-thinking/archive/archive-pdfs/build-better-brics.pdf>. His views on decoupling are contained in 'Cloudy picture as concept of decoupling is put in context', *Financial Times*, 29 July 2009 <http://www.ft.com/intl/cms/s/0/38f238d8-5d05-11dd-8d38-000077b07658.html#axzz3i42K6UXL>.

For an excellent article on O'Neill's creative role, see Gillian Tett, 'The story of the Brics', *Financial Times*, 15 January 2010, available at <http://www.ft.com/intl/cms/s/0/112ca932-00ab-11df-ae8d-00144feabdc0.html>.

On the Outreach Five process, see Andrew F. Cooper and Agata
  Antkiewicz (eds), *Emerging Powers and Global Governance:
  Lessons from the Heiligendamm Process* (Waterloo: Wilfrid Laurier
  University Press, Studies in International Governance Series,
  2008) (Chinese translation: Shanghai People's Publications, 2009).

On IBSA, see Chris Alden and Marco Antonio Vieira, 'The new
  diplomacy of the South: South Africa, Brazil, India and trilateralism',
  Third World Quarterly (2005), vol. 26, no. 7, pp. 1077–95, and Ian
  Taylor, 'The South will rise again? New alliances and global
  governance: the India-Brazil-South Africa Dialogue Forum',
  Politikon: South African Journal of Political Science (2009),
  vol. 36, no. 1, pp. 45–58.

On the dynamics of RIC and SCO in connection to the BRICS, see
  Alexander Lukin, 'Russia's identity dilemmas: BRICS, the G8 and
  the Shanghai Cooperation Organization', in Francis A. Kornegay
  and Narnia Bohler-Muller (eds), *Laying the BRICS of a New Global
  Order: From Yekaterinburg 2009 to eThekwini* (Pretoria: Africa
  Institute of South Africa, 2013), pp. 85–100. The Kornegay and
  Bohler-Muller edited collection also provides excellent background
  on the national perspectives on the BRICS from all the member
  countries.

Chapter 3: A historical departure

The classic text on great power transition is Paul Kennedy, *The Rise
  and Fall of the Great Powers: Economic Change and Military
  Conflict from 1500 to 2000* (New York: Random House, 1987).

For an older but perceptive analysis of the non-West challenge, see
  Hedley Bull, 'The revolt against the West', in Hedley Bull and
  Adam Watson (eds), *The Expansion of International Society*
  (New York: Oxford University Press, 1984), pp. 217–28.

On alternative scenarios for future constellations involving China and
  the United States, see Niall Ferguson, 'Not two countries, but one:
  Chimerica', *The Telegraph*, 4 March 2007, available at <http://
  www.telegraph.co.uk/comment/personal-view/3638174/Not-two-
  countries-but-one-Chimerica.html>, and Geoffrey Garrett, 'G2 in
  G20: China, the United States and the World after the Global
  Financial Crisis', *Global Policy* (2010), vol. 1, no. 1, pp. 29–39,
  available at <http://www.globalpolicyjournal.com/articles/
  world-economy-trade-and-finance/g2-g-20-china-united-states-
  and-world-after-global-financia>.

On the differences between China and BRICS, see Graham Allison, 'China doesn't belong in the BRICS', *The Atlantic*, 26 March 2010, available at <http://belfercenter.ksg.harvard.edu/publication/22906/china_doesnt_belong_in_the_brics.html.

On the debate about the historical importance of the Third World challenge, see Stephen D. Krasner, *Structural Conflict: The Third World Against Global Liberalism* (Berkeley: University of California Press, 1985), and John G. Ruggie and Jagdish Bhagwati (eds), *Power, Passions, and Purpose: Prospects for North-South Negotiations* (Cambridge MA: MIT Press, 1984).

On contemporary analogies between the Third World challenge and BRICS, see Kevin Gray and Craig Murphy, 'Introduction: rising powers and the future of global governance', *Third World Quarterly* (2013), vol. 34, no. 2, pp. 183–93.

On the importance of the Bandung conference, see See Seng Tan and Amitav Acharya (eds), *Bandung Revisited: The Legacy of the 1955 Asian-African Conference for International Order* (Singapore: NUS Publishing, 2009).

On the special features of the newly industrialized countries, see Nigel Harris, *The End of the Third World: Newly Industrializing Countries and the Decline of an Ideology* (London: Penguin, 1987). See also Hans-Henrik Holm, 'The end of the Third World?' *Journal of Peace Research* (1990), vol. 27, no. 1, pp. 1–7.

Chapter 4: Hanging together

For the shift to informalism, see Risto Penttilä, 'Multilateralism light: the rise of informal international governance' (London: Centre for European Reform), available at <http://www.cer.org.uk/publications/archive/essay/2009/multilateralism-light-rise-informal-international-governance>.

For a fuller discussion of these dynamics, see Randall Stone, 'Informal governance in international organizations: introduction to the special issue', *Review of International Organizations* (2013), vol. 8, no. 2, pp. 121–36, available at <http://link.springer.com/article/10.1007%2Fs11558-013-9168-y>. See also Andrew F. Cooper and Asif B. Farooq, 'BRICS and the privileging of informality in global governance', *Global Policy* (2013), vol. 4, no. 4, pp. 428–33, available at <http://onlinelibrary.wiley.com/doi/10.1111/1758-5899.12077/abstract>.

On the start-up phase of BRICS, see Oliver Stuenkel, 'Emerging powers and status: the case of the first BRICs summit', *Asian Perspective* (2014), vol. 38, no. 1, pp. 89–109. See also Luiz Inácio Lula da Silva, 'At Yekaterinburg, the BRICs come of age', *Hindu*, 16 June 2009, available at <http://www.thehindu.com/todays-paper/tp-opinion/at-yekaterinburg-the-brics-come-of-age/article261939.ece>.

On the outlier role of Russia in BRICS, see S. Neil MacFarlane, 'The "R" in BRICs: is Russia an emerging power?' *International Affairs* (2006), vol. 82, no. 1, pp. 41–57.

On South Africa's motivations in the BRICS, see Chris Alden and Maxi Schoeman, 'South Africa in the company of giants: the search for leadership in a transforming global order', *International Affairs* (2013), vol. 89, no. 1, pp. 111–29.

On the connection of rising states to trade, see Andrew Hurrell and Amrita Narliker, 'A new politics of confrontation? Brazil and India in multilateral trade negotiations', *Global Society* (2006), vol. 20, no. 4, pp. 415–33, and Amrita Narlikar, *New Powers: How to Become One and How to Manage Them* (London: Christopher Hurst, 2010).

On the BASIC group, see Kars Hallding, Marie Olsson, Aaron Atteridge, Antto Vihma, Marcus Carson, and Mikael Román, 'Together alone: BASIC countries and the climate change conundrum', Nordic Council of Ministers, 13 October 2011, available at <http://www.sei-international.org/publications?pid=1963>.

For a broader perspective on the BRICS–G20 dynamics, see Andrew F. Cooper and Ramesh Thakur, 'The BRICS in the new global economic geography', in Thomas G. Weiss and Rorden Wilkinson (eds), *International Organization and Global Governance* (London and New York: Routledge, 2014), pp. 265–78.

Chapter 5: Building the New Development Bank

For good background on the general challenges and opportunities for development and governance in the global South, see José Antonio Ocampo, 'Rethinking global economic and social governance', *Journal of Globalization and Development* (2010), vol. 1, no. 1, available at <http://www.degruyter.com/view/j/jgd.2010.1.1/jgd.2010.1.1.1020/jgd.2010.1.1.1020.xml>.

For the potential of rising states to initiate parallel institutions, see
Naazneen Barma, Ely Ratner, and Steven Weber, 'Report and
retort: a world without the West', *The National Interest* (2007),
vol. 90, pp. 23–30.

For a first-rate cluster of articles on national development banks in
the BRICS, see the special section edited by Kathleen Hochstetler,
Global Policy (2014), vol. 5, no. 3, especially her article, 'Development
banks of the developing world: nature, origins and consequences',
pp. 344–5, and the article by Gregory Chin, 'The BRICS-led
development bank: purpose and politics beyond the G20', pp. 363–76.

On the rationale for the NDB, see Adriana Abdenur, 'China and the
BRICS development bank: legitimacy and multilateralism in
South–South cooperation', *IDS Bulletin* (2014), vol. 45, no. 4,
pp. 85–101, and Barry Eichengreen, 'Do the Brics need their own
development bank?' *The Guardian*, 14 August 2014, available at
<http://www.theguardian.com/business/2014/aug/14/
brics-development-bank-imf-world-bank-dollar>.

For the role of think tanks in the development of the NDB, see Samir
Saran and Vivan Sharan, 'It's time for a "BRICS fund"', *Russia
Beyond the Headlines*, 14 December 2011, available at <http://in.
rbth.com/articles/2011/12/14/its_time_for_a_brics_fund_13396.
html>. For a comprehensive analysis of India's optimism about
BRICS, see BRICS, *The BRICS Report: A Study of Brazil, Russia,
India, China, and South Africa with Special Focus on Synergies and
Complementarities* (New Delhi: Oxford University Press, 2012).

For a sample of the media reports on the negotiations on the NDB,
see Alonso Soto, 'Negotiations to launch new BRICS bank at
impasse—sources', *Reuters*, 15 July 2014, available at <http://af.
reuters.com/article/investingNews/idAFKBN0FK1MO20140715>,
and Alonso Soto and Anthony Boadle, 'BRICS set up bank to
counter Western hold on global finances', *Reuters*, 16 July 2014,
available at <http://in.reuters.com/article/2014/07/15/
brics-summit-bank-idINKBN0FK08620140715>.

For the wording of the Agreement on the New Development Bank,
issued at the Fortaleza Summit on 15 July 2014, see <http://www.
brics.utoronto.ca/docs/140715-bank.html>.

Chapter 6: BRICS as the recognition of states, not societies

On state–societal relations within the BRICS, see Rajesh Tandon and
Kaustuv Kanti Bandyopadhyay, 'Civil society–BRICS engagement:

opportunities and challenges' (New Delhi: PRIA and FIM, 2013), available at <http://fimforum.org/custom-content/uploads/2012/06/Civil-Society-BRICS-Engagement-Synthesis-Paper-1.pdf>. For an overview of state–non-state relations in other forms of informal summitry, see Andrew F. Cooper, 'Civil society relationships with the G20: an extension of the G8 template or distinctive pattern of engagement?' *Global Society* (2013), vol. 27, no. 2, pp. 179–200.

For a Russian analysis of the security dimension in the BRICS, see Vyacheslav Nikonov, 'BRICS: analysing the security dimension' (Toronto: BRICS Information Centre, 2013), available from <http://www.brics.utoronto.ca/newsdesk/durban/nikonov.html>.

On the potential for advances in health policy, see John Kirton, Julia Kulik, and Caroline Bracht, 'Generating global health governances through BRICS summitry', *Contemporary Politics* (2014), vol. 20, no. 2, pp. 1–17.

For a critical examination of BRICS in development, see Pádraig Carmody, *The Rise of the BRICS in Africa: The Geopolitics of South–South Relations* (London: ZED Books, 2013).

For signs of a debate about the state-centric nature of the BRICS, see Samir Saran, 'The Africa question', *Indian Express*, 12 December 2012, available at <http://archive.indianexpress.com/news/the-africa-question/1043854/0>. See also Oliver Stuenkel, 'Why BRICS matters', e-international relations, 28 March 2012, available at <http://www.e-ir.info/2012/03/28/why-brics-matters>.

On trade among the BRICS countries, see Brazil's Ministry of External Relations, 'Economic data and trade statistics' (2014), issued for the Fortaleza Summit and available at <http://brics6.itamaraty.gov.br/about-brics/economic-data>.

Chapter 7: The staying power of the BRICS

On the economic challenges to the BRICS ascendancy, see Ruchir Sharma, 'Broken BRICs: why the rest stopped rising', *Foreign Affairs* (November/December 2012), vol. 91, no. 6, pp. 2–7, available from <http://www.foreignaffairs.com/articles/138219/ruchir-sharma/broken-brics>. See also Harsh V. Pant, 'The BRICS fallacy', *Washington Quarterly* (2012), vol. 36, no. 3, pp. 91–105, available at <http://csis.org/files/publication/TWQ_13Summer_Pant.pdf>.

On the geostrategic implications of the BRICS, see the contrasting views of Zaki Laïdi, 'The BRICS against the West?' Sciences Po, CERI Strategy Papers No. 11, November 2011, available at <http://papers.ssrn.com/sol3/papers.cfm?abstract_id=2315108>, and Pepe Escobar, 'The BRIC post-Washington consensus', *Asia Times*, 17 April 2010, available at <http://www.atimes.com/atimes/Central_Asia/LD17Ag01.html>.

On the need for the BRICS to play a bigger role in the global system, see Dani Rodrik, 'What the world needs from the BRICS', Project Syndicate, 10 April 2013, available from <http://www.project-syndicate.org/commentary/the-brics-and-global-economic-leadership-by-dani-rodrik>.

Index